THE MUSIC MAKERS

OTHER BOOKS BY STANTON A. COBLENTZ

Poetry

GREEN VISTAS

WINDS OF CHAOS

THE PAGEANT OF MAN

SONGS BY THE WAYSIDE

ARMAGEDDON

THE LONE ADVENTURER

SHADOWS ON A WALL

THE MERRY HUNT AND OTHER POEMS

SONS OF THE REDWOODS

THE ENDURING FLAME

SENATOR GOOSE AND OTHER RHYMES

THE THINKER AND OTHER POEMS

Prose

THE TRIUMPH OF THE TEAPOT POET

THE LITERARY REVOLUTION

THE WONDER STICK

WHEN THE BIRDS FLY SOUTH

THE DECLINE OF MAN

MARCHING MEN

VILLAINS AND VIGILANTES

THE ANSWER OF THE AGES

Anthologies

MODERN AMERICAN LYRICS

MODERN BRITISH LYRICS

JOHN ACKERSON ● KENNETH SLADE ALLING ● JULIA COOLEY
ALTROCCHI ● LILLAH A. ASHLEY ● JOSEPH AUSLANDER ● ROBERT
AVRETT ● LEONARD BACON ● FAITH BALDWIN ● CHARLES BALLARD
KENDALL BANNING ● ERIC WILSON BARKER ● EVELYN WERNER
BARKINS ● HELEN FRAZEE-BOWER ● JAMES BOYD ● LUELLA
BOYNTON ● BIANCA BRADBURY ● ANNA HEMSTEAD BRANCH
STRUTHERS BURT ● WITTER BYNNER ● MAUD LUDINGTON CAIN
ELEANOR ALLETTA CHAFFEE ● RALPH CHEYNEY ● PHEBE ANN
CLARKE ● STANTON A. COBLENTZ ● ROBERT P. TRISTRAM COFFIN
HOWARD McKINLEY CORNING ● PAULINE AVERY CRAWFORD ● GUSTAV
DAVIDSON ● EDWARD DAVISON ● MIRIAM ALLEN DeFORD ● LeGARDE
S. DOUGHTY ● GILEAN DOUGLAS ● LEAH BODINE DRAKE ● GLENN
WARD DRESBACH ● LUCILLE EVANS ● BRYLLION FAGIN ● ARTHUR
DAVISON FICKE ● SARA BARD FIELD ● MAHLON LEONARD FISHER
HILDEGARDE FLANNER ● OTTO FREUND ● RALPH FRIEDRICH
GEORGIA STARBUCK GALBRAITH ● CLIFFORD GESSLER ● GEORGIA B.
GIERASCH ● LOUIS GINSBERG ● MAE WINKLER GOODMAN ● FRANCES
ANGEVINE GRAY ● ARTHUR GUITERMAN ● DORA HAGEMEYER
AMANDA BENJAMIN HALL ● MAURINE HALLIBURTON ● ELOISE
HAMILTON ● MARION ETHEL HAMILTON ● RUTH GUTHRIE HARDING
ELIZABETH STANTON HARDY ● AMORY HARE ● DONALD WING
HATHAWAY ● KATHARINE SHEPARD HAYDEN ● JESSIE M. HEINER
DuBOSE HEYWARD ● DANIEL WHITEHEAD HICKY ● ROBERT HILLYER
SOPHIE HIMMELL ● DOROTHY HOBSON ● ALMA ELLIS HOERNECKE
HOMER C. HOUSE ● ELEANOR JORDON HOUSTON ● IGNACE M.
INGIANNI ● MARY CECILE IONS ● LESLIE NELSON JENNINGS
JOSEPHINE JOHNSON ● CULLEN JONES ● LEILA JONES ● THOMAS
S. JONES, JR. ● DOUGLAS V. KANE ● CATHLEEN KEEGAN ● JOSEPH
JOEL KEITH ● MINNIE MARKHAM KERR ● INEZ BARCLAY KIRBY
HERMAN EUGENE KITTREDGE ● ALEXA LANE ● LAWRENCE LEE
MARION LEE ● MARY SINTON LEITCH ● JESSIE LEMONT ● WILLIAM
ELLERY LEONARD ● LOUISE LIEBHARDT ● CAROLYN WILSON LINK
LILITH LORRAINE ● BEULAH MAY ● VAUGHN FRANCIS MEISLING
HELLEN GAY MILLER ● J. CORSON MILLER ● EDITH MIRICK ● MINNIE
HITE MOODY ● JOHN RICHARD MORELAND ● THEODORE MORRISON
ROBERT MORSE ● DAVID MORTON ● HELENE MULLINS ● JESSIE
WILMORE MURTON ● JOHN RUSSELL McCARTHY ● ROBERT NATHAN
JENNIE M. PALEN ● DONALD PARSON ● EDITH LOVEJOY PIERCE
HARRY NOYES PRATT ● DOROTHY QUICK ● HUGH WILGUS RAMSAUR
HOWARD RAMSDEN ● LOUISE CRENSHAW RAY ● LIZETTE WOODWORTH
REESE ● CALE YOUNG RICE ● MARGARET R. RICHTER ● CAROL M.
RITCHIE ● JESSIE B. RITTENHOUSE ● GRACE MARGARET ROBERTSON
ALBERTA ROBISON ● E. MERRILL ROOT ● FLORENCE WILSON ROPER
SYDNEY KING RUSSELL ● ARCHIBALD RUTLEDGE ● ARTHUR WILLIAM
RYDER ● ARTHUR M. SAMPLEY ● CLINTON SCOLLARD ● RUBY T.
SCOTT ● ANDERSON M. SCRUGGS ● KARL SHAPIRO ● GRACE
BUCHANAN SHERWOOD ● CLARK ASHTON SMITH ● RICHARD LEON
SPAIN ● CAROLYN SPENCER ● ANN STANFORD ● VICTOR STARBUCK
VINCENT STARRETT ● MARGUERITE STEFFAN ● GEORGE STERLING
WINIFRED GRAY STEWART ● HELEN FRITH STICKNEY ● H. P.
STODDARD ● LEONORA CLAWSON STRYKER ● JESSE STUART
KATHLEEN SUTTON ● ELDA TANASSO ● SARA TEASDALE ● SISTER
M. THÉRÈSE ● NATHANIEL THORNTON ● LUCIA TRENT ● JOSEPH
UPPER ● JUDY VAN DER VEER ● MARK VAN DOREN ● HAROLD
VINAL ● BLANCHE SHOEMAKER WAGSTAFF ● FRANCES REVETT
WALLACE ● TESSA SWEAZY WEBB ● MARY WEEDEN ● EDWARD
WEISMILLER ● WINIFRED WELLES ● JOHN T. WESTBROOK
KATHARINE WELLES WHEELER ● JOHN HALL WHEELOCK ● MARGARET
WIDDEMER ● B. Y. WILLIAMS ● CELESTE T. WRIGHT ● ELINOR WYLIE

THE
MUSIC
MAKERS

An Anthology of Recent American Poetry

Compiled by

STANTON A. COBLENTZ

We are the music makers
And we are the dreamers of dreams . . .
— ARTHUR O'SHAUGHNESSY

GRANGER POETRY LIBRARY

GRANGER BOOK CO., INC.
Great Neck, N.Y.

First Published 1945
Reprinted 1978

International Standard Book Number 0-89609-081-7

Library of Congress Catalog Number 77-094806

PRINTED IN THE UNITED STATES OF AMERICA

INTRODUCTION

I

UNLIKE many compilations, this book does not arise from the labor of a few months, nor even of a year or two. It is the outgrowth of two decades and more of observation and study, not only on the part of the authors represented, but by the anthologist himself. This does not mean that I actually began planning the collection twenty years ago; but it does mean that its basis has been laid, accretion by slow accretion, during a prolonged period. As a reviewer of poetry and as the editor of a nationally circulated poetry magazine, I have had unusual opportunities to sit, as it were, in a watchtower, noting the streams of the country's verse as they flowed in their devious courses. And gradually, with the assurance of a deeply founded conviction, two impressions have forced themselves upon me—two impressions of a sharply contrasting nature, which between them establish a picture of the current poetic scene, and one quite different than would be imagined by a reader without access to the root facts.

The first realization was that, notwithstanding some prevalent assumptions, the age of poetry is not dead. On the contrary, never in the history of American literature has there been such a blended eloquence as we have witnessed during the past quarter of a century, such an outpouring of diverse talents, such a numerous chorus expressing themselves lyrically, passionately, picturesquely, gravely, ironically. From every section of the country, and to the accompaniment of every variety of instrument, the singing voices have burst forth: sonnets and ballads, elegies, odes, performances in blank verse and songs in many strains have been offered not occasionally nor spasmodically but in continuous uplifted harmonies.

But as by degrees I perceived this truth, a co-relative recognition dawned over me. This was that, while many skilled voices were raised, comparatively few were heard, and only a small minority of those few received anything like their due audience. Their works, when they saw periodical publication, usually appeared in newspapers, or in obscure journals of slight circulation; when they attained to the dignity of book format, they were issued in limited editions by small presses that could not afford to publicize them, or in scarcely larger editions by leading publishers that did not find it worth their while to advertise slender individual collections, and that in any case could not break down the reluctance of dealers to storing and displaying such items. Even at best, as I observed, the number of published volumes of capable poetry was not great compared with the amount of such poetry being written; indeed, to mention the names of several strikingly able contributors to this volume, writers such as Minnie Hite Moody, Judy Van der Veer, Cathleen Keegan, Otto Freund and Hugh Wilgus Ramsaur could contribute of their best for years to the magazines without making their bow before poetry's book-reading audience.

Correspondingly, I noted that many even of our better-known poets did not enjoy a public matching their merits. Every reader of current verse will recognize, for example, the names of Arthur Davison Ficke, Robert Nathan, Cale Young Rice, David Morton, Witter Bynner, John Hall Wheelock and Jessie B. Rittenhouse; but how many have stopped to consider that these authors may have written poems deserving to be read and remembered a hundred years from now? How many have wondered if William Ellery Leonard's *Two Lives*, issued a score of years ago, may not be among the immortal long poems of the language? How many have asked themselves if, in the whole history of American literature, any sonneteer has written more nobly or any lyricist more tenderly than George Sterling, who died in 1926? At best, little more than a half recognition crowns many who are regarded as among the most soundly established of recent American poets; a half recognition of occasional praise and publication, but of small audiences.

But stop! the reader will cry. What of the celebrated books by celebrated writers, issuing in a trumpeted stream from the founts of the great publishing houses? What of the Eliots, the MacLeishes, the Marianne Moores, the e. e. cummings? What of Stephen Vincent Benét with his *Western Star*, and William Rose Benét with *The Dust That Is God*, and Kenneth Fearing with *Afternoon with a Pawnbroker*, and Horace Gregory, and Marya Zaturenska, and a dozen others, including Pulitzer Prize winners and recipients of Shelley Memorial Awards and other honoraria? To deal adequately with all these would require the space of a separate critical essay, but this at least may be appropriately said at this point: whatever we may hold as to the merits of these writers and of the school or schools which they represent, we must acknowledge that a great part of their work can not be classified as poetry by the older standards: its rhythms are not those of the older poetry, its subject-matter and its mood are not those of poetry as formerly identified. When an offering can be defended as poetic on the ground that it gives a perfect imitation of a drunkard at a bar (as in the case of a recent critical note in one of our most widely circulated literary media), we have entirely discarded the judgments and the measuring rods of the past.

The fact in itself might not be utterly damning; but what is utterly damning is that those who refuse to accept the newer judgments and measuring rods are in danger of suffering an eclipse. Unless literature is to become as narrow as a proselyting religion, there is assuredly room for more than one school of thought and one current of expression; yet apostles of the newer and "freer" methods in poetry have tended to a monopoly, have been inclined to take

unto themselves the lion's share of the publicity and ap-
plause, and to crowd out those who do not believe as they
do, and who do not write as they write. The result has
been pernicious in two directions: first, that even the out-
standingly capable poet, if he does not choose to endorse
the latest theories and practices, will find himself in peril
of being obscured if not elbowed off the scene; and, sec-
ondly, that the reader who prefers verse of the traditional
singing variety, and who does not welcome obscurity for
the sake of obscurity nor eccentricity in any form, will be
alienated and driven back to the classics or to prose since
he will not know where to find what he seeks amid the
labyrinths of the current output. It is the combination of
these two factors that, in my opinion, makes the present
compilation necessary.

II

The particular selections, as in the case of every anthology,
must depend to a large degree upon the element of per-
sonal taste—the individual predilections, aversions, sym-
pathies, appreciations, perceptions, limitations, subconscious
promptings and life-perspective of the editor. This is inev-
itable; and since there is nothing that can be done about
the fact, it will suffice merely to mention it in passing. One
must not conclude, however, that the anthologist need let
himself be blown whither the wind goes. In so far as was
possible, I have tried to be guided by certain definite con-
ceptions as to what poetry is, and what it should accomplish;
and these conceptions may be summarized as follows:

(1) True poetry must have a rhythmical base, a singing
undercurrent. Ordinarily, though not necessarily, this takes
the form of a measured meter; but in any case there must
be a swing, a flow, a musical pulsation that is different from
and more regular than the rhythm of prose, and that bears
the reader along with a harmonious modulated movement
that subconsciously emphasizes the thought and perpetuates

the impression. It is precisely this movement that a great part of modern verse lacks, in what I have elsewhere called "buzz-saw" rhythms; and because it lacks this movement it leaves something within the reader profoundly unsatisfied, and fails to make a lasting appeal.

(2) Even the most skillfully executed rhythm is like a body without a soul unless poetry possesses a second element, one difficult to define and yet not hard to identify, the quality that most vitally distinguishes poetry from prose, that intangible pervasive essence variously known as "wonder," "magic" and "enchantment." In part this consists of the ability to create an illusion in the reader's mind, and therefore it is of the substance of "faëry lands forlorn," of "The light that never was on sea or land," and of the "Xanadu" and the "stately pleasure dome" of Kubla Khan. Yet often it has its seat in homely things; it was known by Wordsworth when he "wandered lonely as a cloud," by Burns when he sang with a natural simplicity, "O were my love yon lilac fair," by Shelley when he addressed the west wind as "Thou breath of autumn's being, Thou from whose unseen presence the leaves dead Are driven like ghosts," by Masefield when he pictured roses as "Those blood drops from the burning heart of June." This element of magic or enchantment, in a word, is that which principally raises poetry above prose, that which illuminates it and transfuses it with charm and splendor, that which lifts the mind of the reader above the rut of the humdrum and gives him wings. Graphic realistic writing and profound philosophy no less than the most airy nothings may all be graced with this illusive essential, but no amount of thought, experience or application will make poetry of the work that lacks it.

(3) Poetry may have both a satisfying rhythm and the touch of magic, and yet not be completely appealing if it be without a third factor, which for want of a better term we may call clarity. This is not to say that it need have the simplicity of a kindergarten exercise; complex themes by

their very nature require complexities of utterance; yet since the purpose of all expression is communication, whether of a thought, a mood or an emotion, the consummate writer in any field will phrase his messages as clearly as is consistent with their thorough presentation. In other words, he does not seek obscurity as an end in itself, but regards it as an obstacle to be surmounted, a barrier between him and his reader. Consequently, while lucidity alone is not enough —for one could be lucid as crystal, and yet unpoetic as an oily rag—the writer who does express himself with greatest clarity is likely to make the deepest and most direct appeal to the feelings, the imagination and the emotions of his readers.

III

These, then, are the standards by which I have sought to be guided in making the selections for the present volume. Not that I could hope always to succeed unless ruled by an almost superhuman perfection; but my intention, in any case, has held firm: to bring out that element of lyrical strength which is so abundant in current writing and yet relatively so neglected in most compilations.

Several explanations, however, must be made. One is as to the scope of the anthology. Because of the vastness of the field, I have limited my selections to the continental United States, regretfully omitting all work of Canadians and overseas writers. And because some demarkation in time is necessary, I have aimed to confine my selections to work first published since January 1, 1924; not only because the period of over twenty-one years covers approximately a generation of poets, but because the choice of this date makes it unnecessary for me to encroach on the territory of my *Modern American Lyrics*, published in 1924. In some few instances I may unknowingly have stepped beyond my self-established boundaries; and this applies particularly to cases in which poems were privately printed or in which I have drawn from "selected" or "collected" works republished in part from out-of-print volumes first issued before the prescribed date. But such exceptions, if they occur, can be of little significance.

It is not impossible that the reader, in thumbing through these pages, will find his favorite author to be missing, and for this reason some further explanations are in order. For one thing, it has seemed to me that it would serve no purpose to include certain writers, such as Edwin Arlington Robinson, Edna St. Vincent Millay and Robert Frost, whose best work has already been anthologized almost *ad nauseam*. And, for another thing, I was unable to escape the inevitable limitation of all contemporary anthologists: that they can not possibly know every poet, can not conceivably have seen every poem, and by sheer inadvertence or misjudgment may have neglected the very figures whom the future will hold most worthy of respect.

Last of all, there is the powerful restriction of the copyright laws, because of which it has not been possible to represent every writer whom I would have liked to include, nor to offer as many selections as I desired by certain poets who do contribute to these pages. Yet I can testify that this obstacle has, on the whole, had comparatively little effect, owing to the kindness and co-operation of the authors and their publishers. For the reprint permissions that made this collection possible, I have the following to thank:

Caxton Printers, Ltd., for selections from *Streams from the Source,* by Helene Mullins.

Creative Age Press, Inc., for excerpts from *The Two Persephones,* by Robert Morse.

Thomas Y. Crowell Company for selections from *Notes of Death and Life,* by Theodore Morrison.

Dorrance and Company for a selection from *This Unquenched Thirst,* by Minnie Markham Kerr.

E. P. Dutton & Company for selections from *Death and General Putnam,* by Arthur Guiterman, and for a selection from *Autolycus in Limbo,* by Vincent Starrett.

Farrar and Rinehart, Inc., for selections from *Last Poems of Anna Hemstead Branch, Jasco Brown and Selected Lyrics,* by DuBose Heyward, and *Hill Garden,* by Margaret Widdemer.

Fine Editions Press for selections from *Half the Music,* by Bianca Bradbury; *Mill Talk and Other Poems,* by Leslie Nelson Jennings; *From Invisible Mountains,* by Mary Sinton Leitch, and *Where Stillness Lies the Deepest,* by Jessie Lemont.

Harper and Brothers for selections from *Guinea Fowl and Other Poultry,* by Leonard Bacon; *Collected Poems,* by Edward Davison, and *In This Our Day,* by Edith Lovejoy Pierce.

Henry Holt and Company for a selection from *Bright Harbor,* by Daniel Whitehead Hicky.

Bruce Humphries, Inc., for selections from *Sonnets from a Hospital,* by Pauline Avery Crawford; *Afternoons in Eden,* by Amanda Benjamin Hall; *Sonnets and Lyrics,* by Katharine Shepard Hayden, and *The Dark Gaze,* by Elda Tanasso.

Kaleidograph Press for selections from *Drum Beats,* by Kendall Banning; *The Unwilling Gypsy,* by Josephine Johnson; *Newry,* by John Richard Moreland, and *A Kiss for Judas,* by Florence Wilson Roper.

Alfred A. Knopf, Inc., for selections from *Selected Poems,* by Witter Bynner; *Collected Poems of Robert Hillyer, A Winter Tide and Selected Poems,* by Robert Nathan, and *Collected Poems,* by Elinor Wylie, all reprinted by permission of Alfred A. Knopf, Inc.

The League to Support Poetry for selections from *Core of Fire,* by Kenneth Slade Alling; *There Is Still Time,* by Carolyn Wilson Link, and *Rock and Cumulus,* by Richard Leon Spain.

The Macmillan Company for a selection from *Collected*

Poems, by Robert P. Tristram Coffin, and two selections from *Collected Poems,* by Sara Teasdale, by permission of The Macmillan Company, Publishers.

Oxford University Press for three selections from *Poems to Vera,* by George Sterling.

Packard and Company for a selection from *Dawn Is Forever,* by E. Merrill Root.

G. P. Putnam's Sons for selections from *Spider Architect,* by Mary Sinton Leitch, and *Harvest,* by David Morton.

Reynal and Hitchcock, Inc., for a selection reprinted by permission from *V-Letter and Other Poems,* by Karl Shapiro, copyright 1944.

Charles Scribner's Sons for selections from *Eighteen Poems,* by James Boyd; *When I Grow Up to Middle Age,* by Struthers Burt; *Summer Goes On,* by Lawrence Lee, and *Poems, 1911-1936,* by John Hall Wheelock.

Alan Swallow for selections from *Mortal Hunger,* by Gustav Davidson, and *In Narrow Bound,* by Ann Stanford.

University of California Press for a selection from *Original Poems Together With Translations from the Sanskrit,* by Arthur William Ryder.

University of North Carolina Press for a selection from *Color of Steel,* by Louise Crenshaw Ray, and for the selections from *Saul, King of Israel,* by Victor Starbuck.

Viking Press, Inc., for selections from *Two Lives,* by William Ellery Leonard, copyright 1925, by B. W. Huebsch, Inc., and from *Blossoming Antlers,* by Winifred Welles, copyright 1933, by permission of the Viking Press, Inc.

Wagon & Star Publishers and Dion O'Donnol for selections from *Tropic Earth,* by Clifford Gessler, and *Bright Meridian,* by Lucille Evans.

The Wings Press for selections from *Passing Summer,* by Lillah A. Ashley; *The Planetary Heart,* by Eric Wilson Barker; *Green Vistas* and *The Pageant of Man,* by Stanton A. Coblentz; *Heart's Wine,* by Douglas V. Kane, and *Flame Against the Wind,* by Florence Wilson Roper.

Yale University Press for selections from *The Deer Come Down*, by Edward Weismiller.

The Atlantic Monthly for the selection by Luella Boynton.
Florida Magazine of Verse for the selection by Ruby T. Scott.
Harper's Magazine for the selection by Robert Avrett.
Household Magazine for the selections by Jesse Stuart.
The Poetry Chap-book for a selection by Glenn Ward Dresbach.
Trails for the selection by Mary Weeden.
Virginia Quarterly Review and Mrs. A. C. Dietrich for the selection by Lizette Woodworth Reese.
Wings, A Quarterly of Verse for the selections by Mary Cecile Ions, Alexa Lane, and others.

Julia Cooley Altrocchi for *The Dreamers of Death*.
Joseph Auslander for selections from *More Than Bread* and *Riders at the Gate*.
Faith Baldwin for selections from *Sign Posts*.
Evelyn Werner Barkins for a selection from *The Magic Pod*.
Helen Frazee-Bower for selections from *Inner Pilgrim*.
Eleanor Alletta Chaffee for a selection from *Temporary Truce*.
Howard McKinley Corning for selections from *The Mountain in the Sky*.
Miriam Allen DeFord for *Carthage*.
Glenn Ward Dresbach for selections from *Cliff Dwellings*.
Arthur Davison Ficke for selections from *The Secret and Other Poems* and *Tumultuous Shore and Other Poems*.
Sara Bard Field for the selections from *The Pale Woman*.
Mahlon Leonard Fisher for selections from *Sonnets: A First Series*.
Hildegarde Flanner for the selection from *Time's Profile*.

John L. Foley for selections from *Shadow of the Perfect Rose,* by Thomas S. Jones, Jr.

Louis Ginsberg for selections from *The Everlasting Minute and Other Poems.*

Amanda Benjamin Hall for the selections from *Unweave a Rainbow* and *Afternoons in Eden.*

Ruth Guthrie Harding for the selections from her work.

Elizabeth Stanton Hardy for the selection from *Time in the Turning.*

Amory Hare for the selections from her work.

Jessie M. Heiner for the selection from *Beckoning Paths.*

Sophie Himmell for the selections from *Within the Crucible.*

Dorothy Hobson for the selections from *Let There Be Light.*

Eleanor Jordan Houston for *The Glass Blower.*

Ignace M. Ingianni for the selections from *Songs of Earth.*

Leila Jones for the selections from her work.

Joseph Joel Keith for selections from *The Proud People.*

Inez Barclay Kirby for selections from *River Lights.*

Marion Lee and *Versecraft* for the selections from her work.

Louise Liebhardt for the selection from *Love Is a Thistle.*

Lilith Lorraine for selections from *Banners of Victory* and *Beyond Bewilderment.*

John Russell McCarthy for selections from *For the Morning.*

Minnie Hite Moody for the selections from her work.

John Richard Moreland for selections from *A World Turning* and *The Sea and April.*

Donald Parson for selections from *Surely the Author.*

Mrs. Harry Noyes Pratt for the selections by Harry Noyes Pratt.

Hugh Wilgus Ramsaur for the selections from his work.

Laban Lacy Rice for the selections from *The Best Poetic Work of Cale Young Rice.*

Jessie B. Rittenhouse for selections from her *The Moving Tide* and from *The Singing Heart*, by Clinton Scollard.

Alberta Robison for the selection from *Poems*.

Archibald Rutledge for the selection from *Veiled Eros*.

Arthur M. Sampley for the selections from *This Is Our Time*.

Anderson M. Scruggs for the selections from *Glory of Earth*.

Grace Buchanan Sherwood for the selection from *No Final Breath*.

Mrs. Upton Sinclair for the selections from *Sonnets to Craig*, by George Sterling.

Clark Ashton Smith for the selections from his work.

H. P. Stoddard for a selection from *The Lips Keep Moving*.

Leonora Clawson Stryker for the selections from her work.

Kathleen Sutton for the selections from her work.

Sister M. Thérèse for *To Joan of Arc on D-Day*.

Lucia Trent for the selections by herself and Ralph Cheyney.

Judy Van der Veer for the selections from her work.

Mark Van Doren for a selection from *Collected Poems*.

Harold Vinal for the selections from his work.

Blanche Shoemaker Wagstaff for the selection from her work.

Tessa Sweazy Webb for a selection from *Window by the Sea*.

Katharine Welles Wheeler for a selection from *Filled Flagons*.

B. Y. Williams for selections from *Far Is the Hill*.

The following authors who have kindly added their permissions to those of their publishers or who have granted independent permission for the use of their work: John Ackerson, Robert Avrett, Leonard Bacon, Charles Ballard, Mrs. Kendall Banning, Eric Wilson Barker, Luella Boynton, Bianca Bradbury, Struthers Burt, Witter Bynner, Maud

Ludington Cain, Phebe Ann Clarke, Gustav Davidson, Edward Davison, LeGarde S. Doughty, Gilean Douglas, Leah Bodine Drake, Bryllion Fagin, Otto Freund, Ralph Friedrich, Georgie Starbuck Galbraith, Clifford Gessler, Georgia B. Gierasch, Mae Winkler Goodman, Frances Angevine Gray, Dora Hagemeyer, Eloise Hamilton, Donald Wing Hathaway, Alma Ellis Hoernecke, Leslie Nelson Jennings, Josephine Johnson, Cullen Jones, Douglas V. Kane, Minnie Markham Kerr, Herman Eugene Kittredge, Mary Sinton Leitch, Jessie Lemont, Carolyn Wilson Link, Beulah May, Hellen Gay Miller, J. Corson Miller, Edith Mirick, Theodore Morrison, David Morton, Helene Mullins, Jessie Wilmore Murton, Robert Nathan, Jennie M. Palen, Edith Lovejoy Pierce, Dorothy Quick, Howard Ramsden, Louise Crenshaw Ray, Margaret R. Richter, Carol M. Ritchie, Grace Margaret Robertson, E. Merrill Root, Florence Wilson Roper, Sydney King Russell, Ruby T. Scott, Carolyn Spencer, Ann Stanford, Marguerite Steffan, Winifred Gray Stewart, Helen Frith Stickney, Jesse Stuart, Nathaniel Thornton, Joseph Upper, Frances Revett Wallace, Mary Weeden, John T. Westbrook, and Celeste Turner Wright.

CONTENTS

Contents

Contents

Contents

xxxii   *Contents*

Contents

John Ackerson

John Ackerson, who has spent three years at sea with the United States Merchant Marine during World War II, has described his experiences in a series of unique poems that have appeared in various magazines. His home address is Fair Lawn, New Jersey.

THE BANDAGE IS RED

(North Atlantic Convoy)

Dusk on the convoy, still in ordered lines,
While escorts dart for shadows, and I muse
How absence from my dearest one confines
Dreams to such sweets that none but dreamers lose.
Never before have we two been apart
For more than days, and all my pain aligns
Upon the constancy of her true heart,
And a drear hope, that soon our lips may fuse.
Dusk on the convoy, dusk on my cold life,
And none to hunt the shadows that infest;
Courage I have to meet the open strife,
Gun blasting gun, but here within my breast,
The hurt with melancholy shapes is rife,
Only with dreams of dreams the wound is dressed.

Kenneth Slade Alling

For a quarter of a century the name of Kenneth Slade Alling has been associated with American poetry. His poems have appeared in numerous periodicals; he was one of the editors of a well known verse magazine of some years ago,

Sought separate life and individual breath,
And found upon the outer highway,—death!
Until we grow into your heart again,
Strike root and live with you, we shall know pain,
And all the lonely terrors of our ways,
The disinherited and dismal days,
The suffering selves, the alien entities,
The strange desires and empty destinies.

Restore us deep into your deathless scheme,
Dissolve our little spirits, dream on dream,
Until they blend with wisdom of the trees,
Recurrent flowers and root-eternities.

LILLAH A. ASHLEY

Lillah A. Ashley, who died early in 1944 in Glens Falls,
New York, had for years contributed to metropolitan news-
papers and the poetry magazines, and had been represented
in Moult's, Braithwaite's, and other anthologies. She has left
a posthumous collection of her poems, *Passing Summer*, an-
nounced for publication in 1945.

SOUL, MIND AND BODY

Oh, blame me not if I express but ill
The starry meaning hidden in my clay,
Its quicksilver eludes my human skill,
Flashes its gleam, divides and slips away.
Forgive me that I am not beautiful
Who wear a garment which I did not choose
Of changeful fabric obstinate as wool
That lends itself not wholly to my use.
But pity, too, this body that is brave,

Gallant and patient with its Fiery Guest—
Spark of the Infinite—until the grave
From that stern exigence shall give it rest;
Its simple substance, guileless as a child,
Betrayed, exploited and unreconciled.

JOSEPH AUSLANDER

Although of late he has contributed extensively to the popular journals of vast circulation, Joseph Auslander has long been esteemed by the discriminating few for work that is individual without being eccentric, and original without straining for effect. He was born in Philadelphia on October 11, 1897, graduated from Harvard in 1917, and has been at various times a lecturer in poetry at Columbia University, a consultant in English poetry at the Library of Congress, and the poetry editor of *North American Review*. His books include several volumes of translations, *The Winged Horse Anthology* (compiled with Frank Ernest Hill), and many individual collections of short poems.

MARDI GRAS

To see this flame of life, this flow
Of mass and color, glance and glow
Of slitted eyes and the masked laughter
Behind the dotted domino;

To know that men can make believe
Though despots growl and captives grieve;
That still in brief impossible gardens
The innocent snake can dance with Eve—

This comforts, though it cannot bless
For long a world grown comfortless;

How can the fiddles quench the fire?
How beat the blaze with a spangled dress?

And yet, perhaps, if the whole world rang
With music, if the mad world sang
Suddenly, Rome might cease from burning,
And the battle-axe no longer clang.

For song has saved the world before,
And Momus routed the God of War,
And the flash of sequins, the flare of laughter
Frightened the wolf from the falling door.

THE TOWERS OF NEW YORK

There was a Tower
In the land of Shinar
That flashed for an hour
And fell like a star:
There was a Tower and the babbling of many tongues—
    and none of these are.

Are your towers as well
The sick fruits of fable;
A doomed citadel?
A luxurious stable?
O City, my City, must you also blaze and burn out like
    a Babel?

We have decked you with mountains
Of dreams and despairs,
With stone-and-steel fountains,
With sun-trampling prayers—

We have gouged the moon out, we have marched to the
    stars on white stairs!

We have filled you with people,
Inflamed you with power:
O remember the Steeple
That flashed for an hour
And fell like a star in Shinar—and that was a beautiful
    Tower.

O my City, my City,
So fierce in your pride,
Be fierce in your pity:
For mountains can slide,
And a dream can keep them from falling—and dreams
    without pity have died.

Robert Avrett

Robert Avrett was born on December 1, 1901, in Milam
County, Texas; was educated at the University of Texas, from
which he received his Master of Arts degree in 1928; was a
Harrison Fellow in Romantics at the University of Pennsyl-
vania, 1936-37; and is at present Assistant Professor of
Modern Languages at the Texas College of Mines and
Metallurgy (a branch of the University of Texas). His
reviews and articles have appeared in more than a dozen
publications; and his poems, which are markedly original in
bent although faithful to the classical traditions, have ap-
peared in a number of anthologies and about thirty-five
magazines.

I THINK THAT THERE IS LAUGHTER

I think that there is laughter after death,
But quiet as are footsteps in new snow;
And wordless colloquies that need no breath
To ring more clearly than the sounds we know.
Nor may we vision sorrow as a mesh
Designed to snare none but unwary feet
Still shackled with the bonds of sentient flesh,
But wanting in that ultimate retreat.

Both grief and laughter may be timeless things,
Eternal though intangible as dreams
That drift into the mind as if on wings
Of gossamer, or phantom barques on streams
Descending into consciousness from vast
Horizons out of some pre-natal past.

LEONARD BACON

Students at the University of California of a quarter of a century ago will recall the lanky form and mobile, angular face of one who, by turns waggish and serious, did not fit at all into any established academic mold. Leonard Bacon, Assistant Professor of English, was a severe but capable instructor to the members of his poetry classes, none of whom could have been surprised when, years later, in 1941, Mr. Bacon won the Pulitzer Prize in Poetry. At that time he had long given up teaching; he was living in Peace Dale, Connecticut, and had won a nation-wide reputation as a translator and as the author of a long list of books of poetry, much of it written with a barbed Byronic satire.

AN UNANSWERED QUESTION

I have heard whispers that I cannot speak,
Melodies, whose uncapturable tone
Drifted by starlight out of the unknown,
And left me shaken with beauty, and faint and weak.
And in the midnight when the timbers creak
Dreams have possessed me, greater than my own,
And in my solitary heart alone
I have seen grails I never will dare seek.

Why thunder the incalculable wings
About me so, if I am not to fly;
Why do the voices yet within me cry
Melodious? Why do the wild lights gleam,
And spill strange beauty over common things?
I am not visionary. Do I dream?

FAITH BALDWIN

When the name of Faith Baldwin is mentioned, most
readers will think of one of America's best-known writers of
popular novels. But there are some to whom the name will
signify also a writer of accomplished verse. Though small
in quantity beside her innumerable works of fiction, her
poetry has an authentic and individual character. Her col-
lection of short poems, *Sign Posts,* appeared in 1924.

Miss Baldwin, who was born in New Rochelle, New York,
October 1, 1893, lives on a farm near New Canaan, Con-
necticut.

VIGIL

I think that life has spared those mortals much—
And cheated them of more—who have not kept

A breathless vigil by the little bed
Of some belovèd child; they go, it seems,
Scot-free, who have not known fear-haunted days
And nights of terror, when the dim lamp burns
And shadows menace from the waiting walls,
While Life and Death, majestic, in the room
Gigantic rise above the fret and rub,
The petty prickings of small goads, and all
One has, and yearns to have, is, ruthless, flung
Into a fragile balance.
                Hours pass
While on the thread of weary, childish breaths
The issue hangs. Then, one comes close to God,
Waiting and watching; and the hoping heart
Seems branded with the clutch of helpless hands
That leave long scars.
                And when the turning tide
Bears life upon its slow, triumphant surge,—
When tortured eyes grow calm, and when a voice
Speaks feebly—but speaks again—I think
The watchers' eyes see, radiant, a dawn
Break on a newer world, a world more fair
Than ever world has seemed to them before.
God's mercy is as sunlight in the room;
And hearts that through the endless night were crushed
Between the millstones of despair and hope
Are free to sing.
             Oh, life has spared so much—
And less revealed—to those who have not known
A breathless vigil by some little bed.

MASQUERADE

Today the seasons halted in their swing,
And, breathless, slid to a fantastic pause,
While old enchantments, in their grave clothes, rode,

Witch-wise, the golden broomstick of the wind,
With faint, ironic laughter. And I found
In some gray, cobwebbed storehouse of the mind
Forgotten garments of a regal grief,
The purple trappings of an outlived dream,
Most curiously wrought; and tried them on,
As children, playing in old attics wear
The habits of another age, for joy
In fleeting masquerade.
                 So, for an hour,
I wore my lovely sorrow once again,
And laughed to see where Time, the moth, had fed,
And where the gorgeous dyes of passion paled
To blurred and senseless patterns; how the robe
No longer fell in somber dignity,
But, scantily fashioned to maturer use,
Here bound; and here fell short; and here was rent
By rodent years, with sharp, profaning teeth—
And thus—
           I came to know such tenderness
As mothers feel, who finally put away
With slow, remembering hands, the little dress
The child once wore, who long ago outgrew
Such simple needs, and has forgotten them
In more enduring garments of brown earth
That all the silver needles of the rain
With silken strands of flower light and shade
Eternally embroider and renew.

IN THESE DARK WOODS

In these dark woods no herb of solace grows,—
   No gentle flowers, reaching up to light;
No guidepost stands; and no wayfarer knows
   If there be dawn beyond this secret night.

Deserted fires mark the trail with red,—
  Half-hearted embers, signalling defeat;
And here some soul, adventuring, has fled
  From stone-sharp paths on lacerated feet.

In these dark woods is loss. But elfin birds
  Flute long enchantment from some hidden spot,
And one remembers strange and starry words
  And legendary gestures. Time is not

Nor is there any self. One calls a name,
  Entreating ancient gods; one gathers up
Slim branches for the purple altar flame,
  And pours libations from an onyx cup.

No path leads back. And each must serve his day
In these dark woods, where each must lose his way.

Charles Ballard

Poems by Charles Ballard have appeared frequently in
metropolitan newspapers, the poetry journals and standard
magazines ever since 1920. He is a retired teacher of modern
languages, who served for forty years in New York City. His
home is in Bronxville, New York.

MY BROTHER PLAYED

Your cello was my voice and yours ascending,
Seeking a height that man can never know.
I watched you, tense above a rapt string bending,
And breathed the rhythmic passion of your bow.

Across our imperfect peace the voice of sorrow
Sings on unstilled, in endless threnody.

O will it hush to silence one bright morrow,
When human suffering shall cease to be?

Is there a path to rest, in a tranquil heaven,
Near, or beyond the widest-circling star?
You played with all your soul to the question given—
As if you knew the answer was not far.

KENDALL BANNING

A one-time editor of *Hearst's International, Cosmopolitan*
and other popular magazines, and author of more than a
dozen books in verse and prose, Kendall Banning is perhaps
best known for his works on West Point and Annapolis. Yet
he was a poet of rare grace and facility who, as Richard
LeGallienne declares in the introduction to Mr. Banning's
Drum Beats, belongs as a lyric poet "to the troubadours and
ballad-singers. His songs seem to be made of music and per-
fume, and live in the world of emotion in which thought is
an intruder. In his very music is his meaning."

Mr. Banning was born in New York in 1879, and died in
Fort Howard, Maryland, on December 27, 1944.

LOST EDEN

The old enchantment reigns again,
  The apple blossoms blow,
As once upon another spring,
  Dear love, how long ago!

Your hands once swept this laurel hedge;
  These grasses knew your tread;
Along this lane I walked with you
  Who walk with Death instead.

These woods once echoed to your voice;
　　Upon this sun-swept hill
We, dreaming gold and gallant dreams,
　　Lay wonder-eyed and still.

Our star still spills its quivering lights
　　Into the pool we knew . . .
Tonight, among the silences,
　　I walk alone—with you.

SANCTUARY

Not when your banners sweep the sky
　　And lips of friends your feats acclaim,
Nor when gay youth goes riding by
　　With pulse astir and eyes aflame,
Not when your laughter echoes through
　　The halls of revelry, and men
Accord you praise, my dear, do you
　　Have any need of me.

　　　　　　　　　But when
The garlands wither, and the rust
　　Has silenced lutes that strummed the dance,
And golden dreams have turned to dust
　　Beneath the chariot wheels of chance;
When sorrow sets upon your eyes
　　The trace of frustrate hopes, and when
The lonely heart, in longing cries
　　Out through the night—
　　　　　　　Come to me then!

HEART'S HAVEN

It matters not, when I am dead,
　　Where this dull clay shall lie,
Nor what the dogmas, creeds and rites
　　Decree to us who die.

I only know that I shall tread
  The paths my dead have trod,
And where the hearts I love have gone,
  There I shall find my God.

ERIC WILSON BARKER

In the introduction to Eric Wilson Barker's *The Planetary Heart,* John Cowper Powys pays the tribute of an eight-page salutation to Mr. Barker's "remarkable poems"—poems notable for the lyrical sensitiveness they display and for their responsiveness to beauty.

Born in England forty years ago, the author came to California early in life. For years he was employed in a railroad watch-tower, where he wrote his poems between intervals of flashing signals and turning switches; at present he is a dispatcher of trains at Fort Mason in San Francisco. Despite what might strike one as an unpoetic vocation, he continues to produce his poems, which have appeared in the *Saturday Review of Literature, New York Times, Nature Magazine,* and other periodicals. He has won several literary prizes.

TO LORNA

Now in the sad, leaf-haunted autumn weather,
Restless, along the ancient ways I roam,
Along the paths of old we walked together,
Besides the cypress, and the wild sea foam.

Dark are the seas of autumn, dark and lonely,
And all the skies with golden stars are sown.
Deep is the night, and must I then see only
Your shining eyes, the way your hair was blown?

I have been waiting, Lorna, night and daytime,
Green tides of cypress whisper like the sea
Where we two promised in the western springtime:
I will come back to you, and you to me.

Above the empty shore the gulls are crying
Where the sea its sad and ancient note intones,
And lone the white, deserted sands are lying,
Sea windrow, and the sea-forsaken stones.

And desolate in the dark and autumn weather,
Again along the paths of old I roam,
Along the ancient ways we went together,
Beside the cypress, and the cold sea foam.

POINT LOBOS, CALIFORNIA

I

Here Time is God: his shadow on this land
Lies dark across the cypress and the stone.
He holds the clock of tides within his hand
And sweeps them with a deep, eternal tone.
The wave wears down the adamant: an age
Might mark an inch the patient surges gain;
Engraved by water on a granite page
Are epics of the rock-born Titans slain,
Whose cloudy caverns felt the winds of old
Flow through them, and the tiger-throated sea
Burst at their feet where now the fogs enfold
Only the waves that drowned the cliff-held tree,
Where the doomed cypress from their ancient home
Had heard the thunder deepen in the foam.

II

The stone wears down, the long tides rise and fall,
The infinite grains run slowly through the glass,

The tireless waves assail the granite wall.
Across that scriptured face the ages pass
And write thereon their gouged and pitted score,
Leaves from a book of eons whose vast sum
Shall be as sand on this sea-sculptured shore
Before the last cliff crumble, and become
Lost in the flood; before the final tree,
Sucked from the splintering rock that held it fast,
Gives its huge limbs in thunder to the sea,
Goes down in splendid ruin at the last,
And knows the wind no more, nor hears the dirge
For stone and cypress beating in the surge.

EVELYN WERNER BARKINS

Evelyn Werner Barkins is a resident of New York City, where she was born on April 28, 1918. She is the author of one book, *The Magic Pod*, issued in 1945.

WISDOM

What we have done, is done; and I have learned
That it is wiser to forget the old;
That ashes where great fires once have burned,
Are white, like bloodless lips, and ghostly cold;

Are grayish, shapeless things that bear no mark
To tell what has been buried in the flame:
A dream, that now lies lifeless in the dark,
A man, a hope, a love, without a name . . .

HELEN FRAZEE-BOWER

Helen Frazee-Bower, author and teacher, was born in California, and lives today in Los Angeles. Her work has appeared in most of the better poetry journals, and in *Harper's, Saturday Evening Post, Good Housekeeping, New York Times*, etc. She has been represented in Braithwaite's and Moult's anthologies; and was the first winner of the Robert Browning Award of one hundred dollars, offered annually for work by California writers. She is author of *Beauty for Ashes*, a collection of religious poetry; and co-author, with Joseph Joel Keith, of a volume of verse, *Inner Pilgrim*. Her work, faithful to the older standards, is largely in the sonnet form, and displays the finish of a practiced hand.

THIS IS THE TRAGEDY

God pity eyes that have not seen the dawn,
   Twilight, or shadow, or a wind-blown tree,
But pity more the eyes that look upon
   All loveliness, and yet can never see;
God pity ears that have not caught the notes
   Of wind or wave, of violin or bird,
But pity more that, daily, music floats
   To ears that hear and yet have never heard.

God pity hearts that have not known the gift
   Of love requited, comfort and caress,
But, O God, pity more the hearts that drift
   From love's high moment to forgetfulness.
This is the tragedy of common sense:
To dim all wonder by indifference.

FALLEN TREE

How does it seem, for one who stood alone
   Against cool stars, and felt the night-wind's breath
Up in another world, to lie like stone,
   Hushed in this fallen silence that is death?
You were so living and had lived so long,
   How fares the deep, deep sleep that is decay
For one who was the harbinger of song
   And splintered sunlight on a fairer day?

How does it seem? Oh, is the earth's calm breast
   Comfort indeed for one who battled storms,
And took them standing? Is the long, long rest
   Welcome at last to one who stoops and warms
Cold limbs at earth's bright embers—and forgets?
   Or are these crumbling ruins old regrets?

MOTHER

In life we had not seen her once
   So still nor so well-dressed:
The pale eyes closed, the quiet hands
   Too white upon her breast.

The tragedy of death we found
   Was nothing starkly new,
But just the pathos of worn hands
   With nothing more to do.

JAMES BOYD

James Boyd, one of the best known of recent American novelists, might also have been among our best-known poets, had he concentrated upon his efforts in rhyme. Such, at least, is the impression one derives from his posthumous *Eighteen Poems*, from which the following selection is taken. The author, who died in 1944, won recognition with four novels, including *Drums* and *Marching On*. Born in Pennsylvania in 1888 and a graduate of Princeton, he served as a first lieutenant in the First World War, in which his health was so badly impaired that return to an active life was impossible; and it was this that dictated his retirement to family land in Southern Pines, South Carolina, and his espousal of a writing career.

THE BLACK BOYS

Where chimneys cut the sky
And mill roofs stretch away;
Where plants' blank walls stand high
Between the earth and day,
By woven wire fence,
At guarded wicket gate,
Relaxed and yet intense,
Waiting their known fate,
Through heat and cold, through rain and shine,
The black boys stand in line.

Their hands are curved and thick
As hands of peasants are,
Fitted through years to pick
And hook and axe and bar.
They shift their old work-shoes,
They shift their beaten eyes,
Whisper by ones and twos
And then the whisper dies:
The man is coming who will say,
"No black boys here today."

That is the word they know,
The word each understands,

The black boys turn and go,
Hanging their heavy hands,
Hands that once picked the boll—
Oh, white light paradox—
And gave a singing soul
To string and hollow box,
Rejected now without appeal
By white man's spinning steel.

Down the dead street they go,
The black boys' little band,
A race from long ago
Lost in an alien land.
From steps the women stare;
The children look their thought;
The black boys taste the air
And know that they are caught
Between indifference of the great
And fellow workers' hate.

Our sailors crowd the seas,
Our fliers sweep the sky,
But neither those nor these
Know whom they fight nor why
So long as knowledge mounts,
Through battles lost or won,
That in its true accounts
Our freedom is undone
Not by the foe in distant lands,
But by the black boys' empty hands.

LUELLA BOYNTON

Luella Boynton (Mrs. Edward Young Boynton) was born
in 1906 in Texas, where she still lives. Her poems have

appeared in widely read magazines, including *Harper's, Scribner's, Harper's Bazaar, Saturday Evening Post,* etc. The following selection first saw the light in the *Atlantic.*

PLOVER

There is no sky now for the slender song
Remembering old lost and lovely things.
All tenderness is out of tune and wrong
Under the cloud that hides a falcon's wings.
Here, I shall hold the plover in my hand,
Feeling the rapid heart, the swollen throat.
No one will miss it or could understand
Above the clamor such an alien note.

Cover the nest. Where early wheat has grown
Cowers the speckled body of a bird.
Peace is the only song that it has known;
Love is the only answer it has heard.
Rather be held in silence till it die
Than singing in this unfamiliar sky.

BIANCA BRADBURY

Bianca Bradbury is a native of Connecticut, and graduated from Connecticut College for Women in 1930. She has contributed much verse to the magazines and newspapers; has published children's books and short stories; and is the author of one book of poetry, *Half the Music,* which on its appearance in 1944 was recommended by the Book-of-the-Month Club. This volume, from which the following selections are culled, is notable for the impressions which it gives of country life and creatures.

OLD MAJOR

No one of us can keep him in his stall,
No fettered feet can stop his wandering,
When April walks long the pasture wall,
And his old blood is stirring in the Spring
To the rhythm of the harrow and the plow.
There is a faithfulness in all his ways,
And gaunt and lonely and bewildered now
He plods behind his master and the bays,
And stamps and whinnies all along the lanes
For his own harness and his stony row.
And if some April we shall find his reins
Are gone and his stall empty, we will know
That somewhere past the dim, celestial bars
Old Major plows in faith his field of stars.

COMING BACK TO MOUNTAINS

These quiet lazy mountains are my own,
Because I learned them once through childhood's eyes,
Great towering masses of harsh patient stone
Folded deceptively against the skies
In softness, to the bright horizon's rim.
I can be cynical of many things,
Even of hills if I see over them.
But these, these dark mysterious folded wings
That sheltered one child's loneliness, these guard
Me well and timelessly. Oh, he is blessed
Who learns his mountains young, who finds the hard
Blue arms of God. I love the old ones best,
Being the bluest mountains, changing never,
Somewhere deep in me they sleep forever.

ANNA HEMSTEAD BRANCH

Anna Hempstead Branch, one of the best known of recent American women poets, was born at New London, Connecticut, March 10, 1875; graduated from Smith College in 1897; and gave the rest of her life, until her death in 1937, to literature and to social service at Christadora House in New York. She is the author of a number of books of verse, of which the latest is the posthumous *Last Poems* (1944).

THE POET AND HIS SONG

He cannot forfeit it. Not any power
Can take away his god-like gift of song;
When he is silent then it is most strong.
Think not it is the springtime's passionate flower,
Nor ever think it is the globèd earth
With all its changing seasons, not heaven or hell:
His song is magic and himself the spell
Which sings life in and out from death to birth.
Though he is crucified and done to death
The tomb shall crumble. He shall rise and then
Shall fall in words of fire among all men;
Song is his flesh, his substance and his breath.
At the world's end he shall not be afraid
For he is speech by which all things are made.

STRUTHERS BURT

Known both for his poetry and for his prose, Struthers Burt is the author of close to twenty books. Although much of his life has been associated with ranching in Wyoming, he was born in Baltimore, Maryland, on October 18, 1882; graduated from Princeton in 1904; studied subsequently at Oxford, England; and began his professional career as a reporter for the *Philadelphia Times,* and later as an instructor in English at Princeton. His books have followed one another in a fairly regular succession ever since 1914. At present he spends his winters at Southern Pines, North Carolina, and his summers in Wyoming.

I KNOW A LOVELY LADY WHO IS DEAD

I know a lovely lady who is dead,
A wreath of lilies bound her charming head,
Her cornflower eyes were closed as if in sleep,
And on her lips lay silence gay and deep.

No more the garden where she used to walk
Is filled at dusk with laughter and with talk,
No more the swaying fireflies in their glowing
Lantern to left and right her slender going.

I know a lovely lady who is dead,
And fools say there is nothingness instead.

Nothing of all this loveliness? . . . poor dear.
Beauty is not a matter of a year.

Beauty is like the surf that never ceases,
Beauty is like the night that never dies,
Beauty is like a forest pool where peace is
And a recurrent waning planet lies;
Beauty is like the stormy star that traces
His golden footsteps on the edge of rain,
When beauty has been vanquished in all places,
Suddenly beauty stirs your heart again.

She was the purport of innumerable lovers
Who down some woodland road were glad in May,

When leaves were thick and in the orchard covers
The robin and the chaffinch had their say;
She was the toll of countless men who dreamed;
The small hours heard the scratching of the mice;
In hidden room or tower until it seemed
They stood upon a lonely precipice
And felt a thin clear heady breeze that brought
The truth and peace and beauty that they sought.
She was the breath of myriad mountain pyres
That burned into the blueness of the dark:
Beauty is air and earth and many fires,
Runs with the water, sings with each new lark;
She was a pause upon a road that never ends,
Beauty descended on her, and descends.

I know a lovely lady who is dead,
But she was these, and these are in her stead.

. . . Out of the slime and out of endless sleeping,
Into the grayness of the earlier earth,
Crawled such a creature, blind and helpless, keeping
Some unknown assignation of her birth.
Never she knew what moved her to her trying,
What would not let her be what she began;
Only a voice in the blackness crying,
Only a wish that wished itself a man.
The wish is here, the wish is ever growing,
The winds are here, the winds are ever blowing.

And her sweet youth was part of all this too,
She who would catch and store each moment's aim,
Dawns when she opened windows on the blue,
And midnight when Orion marched in flame.
Kind conversation, merriment and wit,
Old friends who knew her wit was ever kind;
And tea in winter when the logs were lit,

And radiance filled the room and filled her mind.
And dogs, and games, and horses silken-throated,
Along a ribboned road that danced with spring,
When every hedge to greenbrier is devoted;
For to her thinking, all and everything
Was music; and with music, soft and bright,
Often she plucked the echoes from the night.
Her body was a casket white and slim,
I would that I had been her very lover;
Ah, the hushed hours when, she with him,
Her young voice whispered over again and over!

Yet now when evening falls and it is late,
And a thin moon cuts clearness from the west,
And Scorpio, rising by the eastern gate,
Along the rim throws his high sparkling crest,
I am no longer sorrowful but glad
Since I was here when beauty found this niche;
Many a man great loveliness has had,
But none with loveliness has been more rich.
A little, ample space was mine to know
What loveliness is and why it cannot go.

THE PURSUIT

Down the road
Between the trees,
In the new moon time of May,
Lighter than the small light breeze,
Whiter than anemones,
Whiter than shy waterfalls
Where in summer white moths stir,
Slim and clad in mysteries
Was the dim far shape of her.

Music seemed
To underlie

All the silence of the night.
Music which, now faint, now high,
Here and distant, passing by,
Has no sound save in the heart;
And the heart cannot recall
This so faint a melody
When the latter hours fall.

Music faint
And sweeter far
Than the honey-noted flute,
In a place where viols are,
Where long windows make a bar,
Yellow, placid in the night,
And the cypress shadows mark,
And a pool that holds a star,
Some enclosed and secret park.

Blossoms pale
With moon and spring
Lapped the forest edge about,
And there went a magic thing,
Not a breeze nor whispering,
Through the silvery aisles and vales,
Through the meadows where the grass,
Bright with daisies in a ring,
Did not stir to let her pass.

Surely where
Her feet had been,
There would be a secret trace;
Surely when the moon was high
She would turn and show her face;
Surely by some hidden stream
She would pause and rest awhile,
And the water troubled be
With her soft unknown smile.

Swifter than
The nightjar flings
His small body to the moon,
Swifter than the gossamer wings
That the dusk of August brings
Over water-lilied pools,
Swift, and swifter down the hill,
Up where tangled grape-vine swings,
Sped her going, speeds it still.

No pursuing
Feet can win
Ever a glimpse of her shy brow;
Lost the hidden forest in,
Trapped as if with delicate gin,
Sore perplexed the hunter bides;
Till the stars begin to fade;
Till the dawn, where she had been,
Leaves him lonely and afraid.

Witter Bynner

As poet, playwright and editor, as a translator and as a
reader of verse, as a patron of young poets and as instructor
of a poetry group for one notable season at the University
of California, Witter Bynner has engraved his mark deeply
upon the literary consciousness of America. He was born in
Brooklyn in 1881; graduated from Harvard twenty-one years
later; has served as assistant editor of *McClure's* magazine
and as a publishers' literary adviser, and has issued innu-
merable books of poems, plays, and translations from the
French and the Chinese, the latter mostly done in collabora-
tion with Kiang Kang-hu. Mr. Bynner's work reveals an

extraordinary technical skill and facility, as well as mastery of a great variety of subjects. He is at present living at Chapala, Jalisco, Mexico.

A DANCE FOR RAIN

(Cochiti)

You may never see rain, unless you see
A dance for rain at Cochiti,
Never hear thunder in the air
Unless you hear the thunder there,
Nor know the lightning in the sky
If there's no pole to know it by.
They dipped the pole just as I came,
And I can never be the same
Since those feathers gave my brow
The touch of wind that's on it now,
Bringing over the arid lands
Butterfly gestures from Hopi hands
And holding me, till earth shall fail,
As close to earth as a fox's tail.

I saw them, naked, dance in line
Before the candles of a leafy shrine:
Before a saint in a Christian dress
I saw them dance their holiness,
I saw them reminding him all day long
That death is weak and life is strong
And urging the fertile earth to yield
Seed from the loin and seed from the field.
A feather in the hair and a shell at the throat
Were lifting and falling with every note
Of the chorus-voices and the drum,
Calling for the rain to come.
A fox on the back, and shaken on the thigh

Rain-cloth woven from the sky,
And under the knee a turtle-rattle
Clacking with the toes of sheep and cattle—
These were the men, their bodies painted
Earthen, with a white rain slanted;
These were the men, a windy line,
Their elbows green with a growth of pine.
And in among them, close and slow,
Women moved, the way things grow,
With a mesa-tablet on the head
And a little grassy creeping tread
And with sprays of pine moved back and forth,
While the dance of the men blew from the north,
Blew from the south and east and west
Over the field and over the breast.
And the heart was beating in the drum,
Beating for the rain to come.

Dead men out of earlier lives,
Leaving the graves, leaving their wives,
Were partly flesh and partly clay,
And their heads were corn that was dry and gray.
They were ghosts of men and once again
They were dancing like a ghost of rain;
For the spirits of men, the more they eat
Have happier hands and lighter feet,
And the better they dance the better they know
How to make corn and children grow.

And so in Cochiti that day,
They slowly put the sun away
And they made a cloud and they made it break
And they made it rain for the children's sake.
And they never stopped the song or the drum
Pounding for the rain to come.

The rain made many suns to shine,
Golden bodies in a line
With leaping feather and swaying pine.
And the brighter the bodies, the brighter the rain
Where thunder heaped it on the plain.
Arroyos had been empty, dry,
But now were running with the sky;
And the dancers' feet were in a lake,
Dancing for the people's sake.
And the hands of a ghost had made a cup
For scooping handfuls of water up;
And he poured it into a ghostly throat,
And he leaped and waved with every note
Of the dancers' feet and the songs of the drum
That had called the rain and made it come.

For this was not a god of wood,
This was a god whose touch was good,
You could lie down in him and roll
And wet your body and wet your soul;
For this was not a god in a book,
This was a god that you tasted and took
Into a cup that you made with your hands,
Into your children and into your lands,
This was a god that you could see,
Rain, rain, in Cochiti!

MAUD LUDINGTON CAIN

Maud Ludington Cain, a native of Iowa, is the author of
two books and of many magazine verses; has won several
literary prizes; and has given more than a hundred lectures
on poetry throughout the Middle West. Although she started

rhyming at the age of nine, she did not attempt publication until past thirty, when her first effort won an award from a Chicago magazine. Her home is in Marshalltown, Iowa.

TO OMAR KHAYYÁM

(Excerpt from a recent letter from a soldier:
"Today I bought a Pocket Edition of 'The Rubaiyat'.")

Eight hundred years!—and still beneath your vine
You sit, tent-maker, pouring forth your wine—
    The heady wine of wisdom and of wit—
While kings a moment flourish and decline.

The mighty kingdoms and the cavalcade
Of conquerors each one his hand has played,
    Has lost, or pocketed his silly gains,
And then the thrones dissolve, the glories fade.

Eight centuries of Caesars helmeted,
Of fair blood spilled, of wives discomforted,
    Of periwigs and human pawns and woe—
Yet still the garden blooms, the rose is red.

And still they read you—sinner, saint and sage;
And still the young men, summoned to engage
    In wars uncomprehended and unsought,
Re-read, turn down and mark a favored page.

So plain—so plain!—you saw the idle dream—
The pitfall, Power, and its phantom gleam—
    While only Love and Beauty (arms of Truth)
Can bridge the terror of the darkening stream.

For you ambition held no prize, no lure;
You knew the proudest prelate unsecure;
    And craving only beauty, truth and love,
Drank at a spring that flows forever pure.

And still we grope, O dark philosopher!—
The saint no wiser than the reveller—
    Knowing ourselves in veriest shame to be
No nearer heaven on earth than once *you* were.

ELEANOR ALLETTA CHAFFEE

To those who have followed American poetry over a period
of years, the name of Eleanor Alletta Chaffee is far from
unfamiliar. She has long contributed to leading periodicals;
has written and sold articles, children's stories and interviews
in addition to verse; is the author of a book, *Temporary
Truce,* and is at present on the staff of a large national maga-
zine. Her home is in Ridgewood, New Jersey.

NIGHTINGALE

He weeps, who never knew the weight of tears:
His heart, light as a whisper in his breast,
Carries the sorrowing of all mortal years;
Of strange lost wanderers that reach no rest.
In one note spun like gossamer he sings
Whole octaves wrought of griefs he knows not of,
And in the secret stirring of his wings
The night conceals the very thought of love.
Shadow he wears like mail, and shadows hide
The voice that threads the darkness with despair:
Until the dawn comes like an amber tide
This is the likeness that the wood will wear—
Silences linked to silences, like pain
Strung musically along an ebon chain.

RALPH CHEYNEY

Ralph Cheyney, who was born in Philadelphia and died in Harlingen, Texas, on October 15, 1941, has served in various editorial capacities on *Unity, Peace Digest, Horizons,* etc. He has been represented in scores of magazines and in many anthologies, and was conspicuous during his lifetime as a crusader not only for poetry but against social inequality and injustice. He is the author of five books, in addition to four written jointly with his wife, Lucia Trent.

MOTION PICTURE SHOW

Can this, the world we see today, be real?
Oh, sleeper, turn and dream a dream more true
To faith in God's design and manhood's due
Than this shrill fever-fantasy of steel
With men too rushed to think, too massed to feel!
Could Life deprive so many, bless so few?
Our lives are but a shadowplay that you
Need never fear our wakening will heal.

And now when music drowns the slumland din,
Evolves a world not destitution-racked,
I know, while Something Greater looms and yearns,
The curtain that is consciousness grown thin,
The silver screen on which our passions act
The photoplays from which the Spirit learns.

PHEBE ANN CLARKE

Phebe Ann Clarke was born in Vermont in 1914, attended Goucher College, and lives today in Glendale, Ohio. She is the author of one book, *The Innkeeper's Wife,* a Christmas story; and of poems that have appeared in *American Mercury, Christian Century* and other publications.

ALIENS

Dear Love, remember how the saplings clung
Deep-rooted, to the pungent mountain soil
That wombed them when as teeming seeds they sought
The sun? Chainlike their arms spread out around
And down, enfolding earth, until the child
Became the lover. Strength—abounding strong,
Consummate love, and mutual sharing, these
Wedded the forest to its mother-wife.

But mightier passion still raged in the storm:
When lightning twisted cruelly down and wind
Lashed through the woodland, giants sometimes fell.
Ah Love, can you forget the suffering
Of sovereign oaks, their naked roots laid bare
To die a yearning, thirsty death! So bleeds
The sundered, deeply-loving heart.
                                        I think
That nothing savagely uprooted lives;
Nor trees, nor hearts, torn from their native place
Can fully bear transplanting. You and I
Remembering our forest, understand
Since we saw oak trees fall, how mountain men
Becoming prairie-dwellers, hunger so,
And die insatiate in a fertile land.

Stanton A. Coblentz

The compiler of this anthology was born in San Francisco, August 24, 1896. His first position, after graduation from the University of California, was as a writer of daily feature poems for the *San Francisco Examiner.* In 1920 he left for New York, where he remained for eighteen years as a free lance writer and regular contributor of book reviews to the *New York Times, New York Sun, Bookman,* and other periodicals. In 1933 he established *Wings,* the quarterly of verse which he has edited ever since. He is the author of twelve books of poetry and eight of prose and has compiled two previous anthologies, *Modern American Lyrics* and *Modern British Lyrics,* which were reissued jointly as *Modern Lyrics.* His home is in Mill Valley, California.

BETTER THE VASE BE BROKEN

Better the vase be broken, better the incense tossed
To the dust that blots and swallows, and the light and fragrance lost!
Better no winds or waters ever intone my name
Than that I smirch the altar to clutch at the sleeve of fame!

To be the priest that, faithless, tramples the fire to climb!
The painter who slashes the canvas to tickle the styles of a
time!
Who chooses a milkweed or thistle, acclaimed by the market
a rose—
Better the candle gutter, better the story close!

Applause, like a flame, may dazzle, curtseying flattery woo,
Yet how shall a man find comfort, knowing his heart untrue?
How, when his love is given for the spangled harlot's kiss,
Shall he follow the home-lamp's gleaming, bask in the hearthfire's bliss?

Better the bust he sculptured shine for his eyes alone!
Better he seize a mallet and shatter the Phidian stone!
Better the vase be broken, better the incense tossed
To the dust that blots and swallows, and the light and fragrance lost!

MOUNTAIN REVERY

Firm-pillowed on the earth, with head to grass,
And all the hot sky arching over me,
Almost I seem to merge with the great mass
Of root, and rock, and pinnacle, and tree.
Almost I seem to lose the "I," the one,
And blend with currents of the bush and stone,
And with the flowing air, the soil and sun,
And feel no more self-clouded and alone.

Then to the rhythm that the oriole hears,
And to the mountain's green, leaf-fluttering heart,
And to a voice above all hopes and fears,
I am attuned . . . when, worn by men and art,
Firm-pillowed on the earth, with head to grass,
I breathe the enfolding peace that does not pass.

FROM *THE PAGEANT OF MAN*

Patient is time, and gradual are its ways:
The poppy withers, but rekindles still
Though frosts of toothed November numb and kill.
Look! in the blue-and-green of quilted Mays,
She spreads her golden coverlet on the hill,
And all the lunge and dash of rains and gales
Leave her the lovelier when the spring prevails.

Patient is time, and takes no count of loss:
The lightning cares not if five hundred years
Have nursed the oak, when with flame-driven spears
It rends the bole: a tuft of grass or moss
Would seem as worthy tribute to the shears
Of the great Master, for the hours unborn
May rear again what perished hours have shorn.

Patient is time: in its encircling clasp
The worlds are only atoms, and the sweep
Of epochs quiet as an infant's sleep.
It overlooks the evanescent clasp
Of Titans, and the crops that midgets reap,
Since, in its vision, that alone survives
Which dwells unchanged by froth of passing lives.

Patient is time: it knows that truth will stand
Against all tempests, like the iron core
Of the firm earth; that beauty's luminous ore
Shall still remain, though many a raiding hand
Crumble to dust; that love will surge and soar
Across the universe like pulsing light,
Though hatred snarl, wolves prowl, and scorpions bite.

Patient is time!—and what if cyclones slay
With smoke-grim funnels? What if breakers smash
At pillars of the land, and torrents splash
Over the fields, with lips of muddy spray?
That which is real is real, though planets crash
And eons die, and shall endure unchanged
When continents and their oceans are estranged!

❋ ❋ ❋

So be not sad if time seem long and slow.
Too often man, forgetting light and hope,
Is like a searcher at a microscope,
Whose world is an atomic phantom-show.
The master Workman does not halt nor grope,
But builds, and builds, and subtly builds again
In ways unrecognized, unknown to men.

And what the goal, you may inquire in vain,
Though every seed contains the risen bough.
Man, who for ages yet may reap and plow

Through changing forms in an unchanging reign
Of love and labor, and of heads that bow
And straining, sweaty backs, need only ask
If he fulfill his spirit-chosen task;

Need but be true to that High Lord within
Which opens windows to a hidden worth;
For, only so, can he outsoar his birth
As fellow to the mole, the cougar's kin.
And, only so, can he be prince of earth
Beyond the saurian's way, in those weird lands
Where wing-borne lizards flapped in screeching bands.

Brother in form to marmot and baboon,
Yet in his soul a sparkle from the stars!
Perhaps he yet shall burst his fleshly bars,
And, ere this globe turn sapless as the moon,
Ascend, triumphant in heroic scars,
To daunt the angels—but this shall not be
Before new continents assemble from the sea!

Robert P. Tristram Coffin

Pulitzer Prize winner in poetry for 1936, and author of
so many books that it requires a quarter of a column in
Who's Who in America merely to list them all, Robert P.
Tristram Coffin is a living answer to those who maintain that
present-day poetry can not be lucid. His work is deliberately
so simple that a child could understand most of it, and he
turns by choice to the homeliest of themes, many of which
take on a glow beneath his skilled handling.

Mr. Coffin was born on March 18, 1892, in Brunswick
Maine, where he still lives; graduated *summa cum laude*

from Bowdoin in 1915; took his Master's degree at Princeton in 1916; went to England as a Rhodes Scholar; and subsequently taught English at Wells College and Bowdoin and lectured at Columbia University.

AT THE LOWEST EBB OF NIGHT

Now at the lowest ebb of night
　When only snails go by
On silver paths across the lawn,
　There wakes a lidless eye.

Round and lidless as the moon,
　Bulging with its fear,
An angel sitting in the depths
　Of its amber sphere.

The hound's nose lies between his paws,
　The horse stands mute as stone,
Of all the friends there are to man
　Watches one alone.

He sits upon his perch and lifts
　His battlemented head
And hears the pulses of the stones
　And the snail's low tread.

He hears through thickness of the earth
　The golden ball of day
Reach its lowest curve and turn
　On its upward way.

Joy comes up his stiffened neck
　And blows a trumpet sound,
The flowers stir upon their stalks,
　The seeds stir underground.

The cock sets spheres in blood and sap
  Rolling faster on,
Across the thinning stars roll up
  The crystal balls of dawn.

HOWARD McKINLEY CORNING

Howard McKinley Corning, of Portland, Oregon, has written comparatively few poems in recent years, possibly owing to his employment in the United States Maritime Audit Section at the shipyard of the Kaiser Company at Vancouver, Washington. But during the Twenties and Thirties he was among our most generally published poets, and one with a generally high record of performance; he appeared in innumerable periodicals, and in the anthologies of Braithwaite, Monroe, Untermeyer, and others. He has two books, *These People* (1926), and *The Mountain in the Sky* (1930).

THE MOUNTAIN IN THE SKY

Was it the wind they followed?
  Their feet were battered by stones.

Or a far voice that halloaed?
  The desert hardened their bones.

      The creak of leather, the grind
      Of ox-cart wheels, the despair
      Of trails that led them to find
      What wasn't there.

      Sage . . . and a splash of red
      Where the day sank into the sand;

And the living camped with the dead,
West, toward their promised land.

Days . . . and the trails endured;
Nights . . . and these sturdy hearts
Slept with their wills inured
Under their weary carts.

Days . . . and low in the west
Glimmered a drift of snow
Shot with fire at the crest,
And lit with their own dream's glow!

They marched . . . and westward the drift,
A handspan out of the sage,
Assumed and commenced to lift
Over their pilgrimage.

Westward . . . what once was a mote
White in the eye became
A passionate song in the throat—
While the proud heart breaks aflame.

For always the dream burns first,
Whether poet or pioneer;
And the mountain that rose out of thirst
Has completed a hemisphere.

SAGEBRUSHER'S WIFE

Always at evening when a horseman passed
Along the flaming west, the clomping hooves
Lifted a saffron dust that slowly cast
Abroad before the sunset; or the grooves
Of ruts would lift the creaking of the wheels
Of any weary buckboard. From her door,

After the lonely day and her husband's meals,
She'd watch this dusty sorcery lift and pour.

Over the fields it blew, a vapory screen,
Clouding the passing traveler where he went
Remotely lost beyond; while flowed between,
For her, despair, for him, his sacrament;
Dressing a ghostly hungering that came
Only at evening in the dust and flame.

THE LAST HOUND

When the last hound has wearied of his race
Of rounding in the strayed sheep, and his baying
Breaks on the russet peaks beyond their straying,
Silence returns its broken bars to place.
Shepherd and sheep, companioned of the grace
Of the cool hours, and with no clock for saying
By what long watch the stars may be betraying
Body from sleep to yield the gift of space.

There are wide hours where the sleeping brain
Interrogates with stumbling inquiry
Why the dark peaks invade the starry sea,
While man with hands to reach lifts them in vain;—
Till weary of the shepherd-watch with sheep,
Death, that last hound, will round him to his sleep.

PAULINE AVERY CRAWFORD

For sheer heartrending and graphic portrayal of a poignant experience, Pauline Avery Crawford's *Sonnets from a Hospital* (1936) has few rivals within its particular limited field. The author tells us in a prefatory note that the poems were "set down during a period of three years, two of which were spent in a hospital." Apparently the doom of confinement was to follow her even after the book was written, for the last word her publishers have had from her was from the American branch of a Paris hospital, where she was a patient several years ago with a serious leg condition.

THERE IS NO SOUND SAVE THROUGH THE SWELTRY SHEET

There is no sound save through the sweltry sheet
The heart's loud travail at its timeless chore,
Throbbing and churning as great engines bore
Through heaving waves in equatorial heat.
Or is it but the dull incessant beat
Of molten tears along the ghostly floor
Of the lost Past, whereon forevermore
Echo the steppings of departed feet?

There is no sound, save this and whisperings,
Save this and rustlings from the shadowed hall,
Distant and silken as of folding wings,
As the white feet of passing angels fall.
Oh, pass again! sweet sounds, ere silence brings
With everlasting drums the deathless pall!

TO ME WIDE-EYED THROUGHOUT THE ALIEN NIGHT

To me wide-eyed throughout the alien night,
Soft-footed down the corridor you came
And stood beside my bed; so lost the light
I knew not who you were or what your name;
But dim against the whiteness of your dress,
Like unlit tapers at a shadowed shrine,
I saw your fingers lift in tenderness
To move with petal touch along my spine:

Evoking by their vibrance, rhythmic, slow,
In delicate ascent and downward curves,
Sure as the tide's concordant ebb and flow,
Far music on the harpstrings of my nerves.
　　　Your name I never learned, but I shall keep
　　　The memory of the hands that brought me sleep!

SHUT DOORS ALONG THE HALL LIKE
SLEEPING EYES

Shut doors along the hall like sleeping eyes,
Veiling their shadowy secrets I could see;
Nor what dim shapes they sheltered could surmise,
What spirits spent, or in what agony;
Nor through the clouded hours could understand
Why entering angels graciously forebore,
As if restrained by an omniscient hand,
To shut me off—to close my open door.
Of angels what archangel's listening ears,
Attuned to what strange silences of woe,
Hearing the dropping of what phantom tears
From eyelids ever tearless, thus could know
　　　How very long in darkness I had been
　　　Behind a door no one could enter in?

GUSTAV DAVIDSON

For many years the name of Gustav Davidson has been
known to readers of magazine verse. He is the author of
seven books of poetry, as well as of work in the field of
drama and biography; he is the publisher of *Poetry Chap-
book*, and head of the Fine Editions Press of New York,
which specializes in the output of poets. Much of Mr.
Davidson's work has been done in the sonnet form, but some
of his lyrics are among his most successful offerings.

BIRD OF TIME

Tristan and Iseult are dead
These seven centuries and more,
And yet the burning anguish of
Their mortal and immortal love
That never may be comforted
Is with us still, and at the core
Of all the living who have known
Love's flaming instant, glimpsed and flown.

The sea at Cornwall beats upon
The cliff where Tristan long ago
For Iseult died. The summer sky
Still bends o'er lovers passing by
Tintagel in the shimmering sun;
And all the wildness and the woe
Of their last kiss is in the breeze
Blowing from those far Cornish seas.

O Bird of Time upon the bough!
Out of what turmoil, what remorse
Of human passion, human pain
Does that sad music sound again
Through all our yesterdays and now?
And is love's yearning at the source
Of worlds gone down eternity?—
And worlds unending, yet to be?

EDWARD DAVISON

In the minds of many readers, the name of Edward
Davison is associated with the literature of England. Born
in Glasgow in 1898, he early gained prominence as a maga-

zine editor and as a contributor to the *London Mercury* and other periodicals. His right to appear in the present compilation is evident, however, from the fact that he has lived in the United States for twenty years, is a naturalized citizen, and has served for some time as a lieutenant-colonel in the American army. Before he was called by the war, he was Professor of English Literature at the University of Colorado and Director of the annual Writers' Conference. His poems have been widely published; he has several books, of which the latest, *Collected Poems*, was issued by Harpers in 1940.

DON JUAN'S DREAM

The dark Arabian woman of the dream
Burned through her veils upon him till he woke
Out of a sleep within a sleep and spoke—
Who art thou? But she leaned with hair astream
Above him, flashing back against the gleam
Of his proud eyes the poignard of a look
He knew not how to answer or to brook,
And motioned, waving from the dim hareem
The phantom eunuchs, and the silks let slip
Sighing about her. *Come! In me thy quest
Endeth for ever*—clear he heard her—*I
Am she whom thou hast sought.* Fast in the grip
Of sleep he fought and strained toward her breast,
And writhed and wakened. Then he ached to die.

Miriam Allen DeFord

Miriam Allen DeFord, who was born in Philadelphia on August 21, 1888, but has lived for years in San Francisco, has had a lifetime record of literary and journalistic work. She has contributed to biographical dictionaries of British

and American authors; has published stories, articles and
verse in most of the leading magazines; and has written five
books, including one of verse. Her poetry is widely known,
and has appeared in forty anthologies.

CARTHAGE

Sow it with salt where men went to and fro
    Lost in their daily maze of common cares;
      Sow it with salt where rose old trodden stairs
To shrines forgotten; and thrice deeply sow
The wharves whose galleys went as still ships go,
    Cruising and trading, offering rich men's wares.
    Carthage is dead; and night-beasts dig their lairs
Where once her turrets pierced the evening glow. . . .

Words dropped like stars through time's unending space—
    Dido and Hannibal, Sidon and Tyre and Spain—
      Purple and gold and slaves and ivory—
Only these words are left; and Dido's face
    Of anguish when Aeneas sailed again;
      Hannibal's rage; and Cato's enmity.

LeGarde S. Doughty

Among the pines and the red dirt roads of his isolated
home near Augusta, Georgia, LeGarde S. Doughty was until
recently writing his poems and stories; at present, he lives
among the less romantic surroundings of Augusta itself. He
was at one time literary editor of the *Chronicle* of that city;
he has appeared in the *New Republic, Nation, Free World,*
and other well-known magazines, as well as in several an-
thologies; he has issued one small book of verse, while his
first novel was published in the Spring of 1945 under the

imprint of Duell, Sloan and Pearce. In all his writing, he reveals an original and individual turn of thought and expression.

TO A KING SNAKE

(The king snake, harmless to man, feeds on other snakes, including the most poisonous. It kills by constriction.)

I let you flick your sleek fork-lightning spear
Across the contours of my open hand.
There's nothing evil in you; others fear
Only because they do not understand.
   I place you on my desk
And watch your silent, silken slithering.
Others would shrink away from so grotesque
And so bizarre a thing:
To me an exquisite mobile arabesque.
Is there no elegance in these
Rippling white and jet peripheries?—
Or do men fear your sting?—
Then they abuse you
Because they so confuse you;
A thread of pearls were no less poisoning.
   Fascinated utterly I look
As you wreathe your coils to nothing unholier
Than a living labyrinthine Grolier
On the artless cover of a dusty book.
   I take you up and feel your cool curves weave
Around my wrist and swiftly up my sleeve,
And round my neck. You speak a little hiss;
And in the constant jewels of your eyes
You mirror mine. What friendlier bond than this!
Then what is there about you to despise,
O willing strangler of the copperhead?
   Now quick with smooth and flexile rhythms you go
Down to my breast and coil and make your bed:

Much like the inner flow
Of ink from some tremendous printed page
Down to my heart. And many a lonely sage
Broadly maligned, thuswise has nested there.
But men see ill in friendly things and fair—
Alike the serpent and the printed page. . . .

PALIMPSEST

O Master Scribe, in all your manuscript,
Why will you let no word that's written stay,
But every drop of ink through aeons dripped,
Has gone, is going, and shall go away?

And this that was the horn-tip of an ox
Is now the amber petal of a rose.
It soon will fall among dissolving rocks,
A crinkled wisp; and after that—who knows?

And once there was an erg of energy
Tossed willy-nilly on the ravelling foam,
A germ of empire shoreward from the sea;
But now there is no Romulus, no Rome.

And once there was a macrocosm of fire
Turned decimals in squadrons infinite.
And whither moves the narrative desire?
And what of us who glibly read of it?

O Master Scribe, put down and then erase
Clods, planets, constellations, and the rest—
All are as transient as a pretty face,
For all are an eternal palimpsest.

GILEAN DOUGLAS

One of our newer poets, Gilean Douglas has appeared in
many verse magazines and metropolitan newspapers, and in
Thomas Moult's *Best Poems of 1943*. Several of his poems
have been put to music and published; and in all his work
there is not only a musical quality but a feeling that makes
him one of the most promising of recent arrivals. Formerly
of Reno, Nevada, he is now in Vancouver, British Columbia.

AUTUMN IN WARTIME

I can remember how the autumn came
Striding along the old marked trails we knew,
With all the sky a deep, heart-stirring blue
And all the woods a glory of wild flame.

I can remember the great fires of dawn
Burning upon high hearths of mountain snow,
Cleaving with flaming brands the mists below
And lighting the dark paths where night had gone.

I still can see, a picture clear and rare,
The wild geese black against a sunset sky
And hear the far, shrill cadence of their cry
Beating like wings upon the still, dusk air.

But here the autumn is a dry, sucked bone
Flung down for dreams to starve themselves upon
And I am like a ghost, heartsick and wan,
Searching in mud for stars that I have known.

LAST LEAVE

How tenderly it goes, this farewell day,
How gently lie

The shadows of the tamarack and pine
Upon the sun-washed lake. This is farewell;
This is a last good-bye.
For me no more will silver poplars shine
Against the dusk or brightened clouds foretell
A brighter dawn. How strangely beauty may
Redeem and crucify.

LEAH BODINE DRAKE

Leah Bodine Drake, a native of Lexington, Kentucky, was educated at Hamilton College for Women in her home town, and also at the Kendrick School for Girls in Cincinnati. Since childhood she has written fairy tales and poetry, and within the past ten years she has made poetry a major part of her life. Apparently she has a rare feeling of altruism toward her fellow poets, for her ambition is "to run a poetry magazine and pay the poor, underdog race of poets about two hundred dollars for each poem!" Her own poems, which have appeared in the *Atlantic, Cornhill* of London and the *Saturday Evening Post* as well as in several anthologies, are characterized by their freshness and originality and by their rare play of fancy, which frequently revolves about animals.

FANTASY IN A FOREST

. . . *"And it is well known that the Unicorn by touching the water with his Horn, doth render it free from Poison; and the Creatures of the wild putteth their trust in him, and do Drink thereof."*
—*Beastiary of Amelius of Gault.*

Between two unknown trees I stood
Within an Abyssinian wood.
Unseen beside a cold pool's brink,

I saw the beasts come down to drink,--
The elephant, the shy gazelle,
The leopard in his painted fell,
The camel coloured like the sand,
The serpent like a burning brand,
The horse, giraffe, the red baboon
Down from the Mountains of the Moon,
The zebra striped with light and shade
Beside the lion, unafraid.

Around the pool they took their stand;
I could have touched them with my hand!
No creature moved, no creature leapt,
But all a curious silence kept,
And nothing in the forest stirred;
They waited as if for a word.

Then stepping lonely from the wild
He came, the white, the undefiled,

With ivory hoof and pearly horn,--
The one, immaculate Unicorn!
Moving serenely to the pond,
Bending no blade nor ferny frond
Beneath the quiet of his tread;
He dipped his proud and lovely head,
And that dark fountain's veil was torn
By the sharp splendour of his horn.

Around the circle went a sigh
As if a breeze were passing by;
And then beside the curving brink
I saw the creatures crouch to drink
Those waters cleansed and strangely blest
By that unhuman exorcist.

They drank together, shy gazelle,
The leopard in his painted fell. . . .

I saw these things the day I stood
Lost in that Abyssinian wood.

THE ASSYRIAN LION

We see him sculptured in each ruined hall,
    The hunted lion!—side transfixed by spear,
    Wide, anguished jaws, the body strained to rear
Upon the merciless princes but to fall.
Slaughter unceasing! Thus the lions all
    Perished in stone, once symbol of the fear
    That haunted man: the Desert crouching near,
Lashing his tail beyond their hard-won wall.

And yet the Lion triumphed in the land . . .
    Time is a foe that does not warn nor wait:
    The conquered cities of the hunters saw
The waste-land come with lion-colored sand,
    Springing at last through every crumbling gate,
    To swallow them in one vast, golden maw!

GLENN WARD DRESBACH

For many years Glenn Ward Dresbach has been turning
out his poems steadily, unostentatiously, and without con-
cession to the forces of formlessness and obscurity that have
engulfed so many of his fellow writers. His name is known
wherever American magazine poetry circulates; he has been
represented in many anthologies, and is the author of a
number of books, including *Selected Poems* (1931). For
the past twelve years he has devoted his entire time to the

completion of his *Collected Poems*, which awaits publication as soon as post-war conditions permit. He is a resident of Eureka Springs, Arkansas.

REQUIEM

Not for the dead who fell that dreams may stand
Above the trodden dust, this requiem . . .
But for the failures in the heart and mind
Of men who did not stay the bloody hand
That grasped in plain light all things dear to them;
Not for clear eyes that faced death but the blind
Who tapped the cane on hollow stone to this
Red chaos swirling up from a thundering world-abyss.

Not for the dust of cities from which rise
The towers brighter now than when they fell,
This requiem, but for the flimsy spires
Of selfishness and tenements where lies
Had gnawed like rats; for all who cried "All's well"
When at the walls were nibbling those first fires
The madmen set to test how much we dared;
Not for the courageous dead but the faltering unprepared.

Not for the sunken cities, the twisted shapes
Of beaches of the world, but for the charts
Omitting black rocks, shouldering the spray,
This requiem, for casual escapes,
The urge to profit in accustomed marts
Where profits turned an anguished price to pay . . .
Not for the dead who live forever by
All treasured things they saved—but that they had to die.

DESERT BURIAL

Here where we found him sleeping let him lie,
In this vast tomb whose canopy of sky

Rests on the mountain pillars that have caught
The rainbows whose enchanted ends he sought.
For though we hollow here the tawny sands
And smooth them on closed eyes and folded hands
And pile a little mount of desert stone
We change not his inheritance, alone
In his majestic vault of pillared haze,
Beyond our mortal vision. At his head
A mountain stone of misted gold and red
Into the sun-flecked blue of heaven blurs
And mingles there; orchestral music stirs
Through seven cedars at his feet. . . . Strike deep
His worn prospecting pick in sands of sleep
And let it stand beside him, sign of one
Who sought for mines of gold and was not done
When gold was found, but wandered on and on
For treasures poured from cauldrons of the Dawn.
His moping burro-train finds kindly grass
Beside the water-hole. Let burdens pass
From these hunched shoulders while the patient eyes
Watch for the one who left them to surmise—
Like one who walks a ridge against the blue
Of distance and steps down and goes from view.

ANT BATTLE

The armor of ants is bright in the sun.
The lances flash as the columns run
Into the battle where warriors pile
Deep in a lane of the camomile.

They fight to clear a patch before
The columns that come with a plundered store
Of leaves they forage, before the chill
Creeps down on them from the hazy hill.

Such fierceness out of the things so small!
Such strife with never a crowding wall!
And backs that only death has freed
Of loads commensurate to greed! . . .

We ponder long on the path, unseen ·
By insect madness, and over the green
What shadow falls? And we cannot see
One who is watching you and me!

LUCILLE EVANS

The poems of Lucille Evans have been appearing for
about twenty-five years in verse magazines and elsewhere,
but her work was never collected in book form until the
appearance in 1944 of *Bright Meridian,* from which the fol-
lowing are selected.

THE STARS LEAN CLOSE

Tonight the stars lean close, as though aware
of earth's cold terror. Scintillant and white,
their beams have raced through ebon lanes of light
to touch the anguished ones. The very air
flows tremulous with hope, and man may dare
to lift his eyes beyond the cosmic blight
to where Orion burns, where Vega's light
vies with the timeless flame of high Altair.

Lean closer still, white brothers of the earth!
Unleash your cleansing winds and let them sweep
away the venomous wrongs, the aching scars—
send us a mighty dream of man's rebirth,
a proud, bright vision that the soul may keep,
and bid us claim sure kinship with the stars!

WHITE ANEMONE

I keep in memory one lovely hour
That stirs my heart through darkened days and fair;
Faint with the struggle to escape the snare
Set by the world's grim, vision-crushing power,
By chance I found a garden where a flower,
Gold-chaliced, raised its face in fragrant prayer
In its own petaled shrine, and kneeling there,
Felt my bound soul fly from its grief-barred tower.

Since I have found the path to beauty's place
My peace-enamored self shall never know
Again the haunted cells of loneliness.
For I have looked upon an angel's face
Incarnate in anemone's pale snow,
Fair as a spirit, and as passionless.

BRYLLION FAGIN

Bryllion Fagin, a member of the English faculty of Johns Hopkins University, has published two biographies, an anthology of short stories, a text on short story writing, and a collection of his own short stories. His poems have appeared in numerous periodicals and anthologies.

ON REREADING SHELLEY

And still the night of history gives birth
To Ozymandias, king of kings, who stains
With blood the precious greenness of the earth
To build himself upon the bleaching plains
A lone colossal wreck! His shining sword
Is mighty; mightier still his arrogance

And greed. But not so mighty as the sword
Of poet, dead or quick—a wingèd lance
That pierces armor plate and towering tomb.
Not all the fires in cheering flag-draped towns
Can still the bardic prophecy of doom:
And dust upon the beaches or the downs
Shall mantle Ozymandias soon or late.
There is no silencing a tyrant's fate.

ARTHUR DAVISON FICKE

Arthur Davison Ficke, one of our most distinguished living poets, won recognition years ago for *Sonnets of a Portrait-Painter* and other volumes. He was born in Davenport, Iowa, in 1883; taught English at the University of Iowa; and subsequently earned his living as a lawyer in Davenport. During the First World War, he served for two years in France, and emerged with the rank of lieutenant-colonel; since then, he has lived in the Berkshires at Hillsdale, New York, with his wife who is a painter, and with few neighbors except the naturalist Alan Devoe and the poet Edna St. Vincent Millay.

Mr. Ficke's writing, which includes more than a dozen books of poetry, is notable for the depth of its insight. Some of his best work is contained in his latest book, *Tumultuous Shore*, of which he writes to the compiler: "Perhaps it will interest you to know that the whole basic feeling of that book was born in me as a result of an intensive study of ancient Chinese landscape painting which has absorbed me of recent years; I find in that painting such an exalted and integrated view of the relation of man and nature as does not exist elsewhere in man's long efforts to understand himself and his universe."

SONNETS FROM *TUMULTUOUS SHORE*

II

I walked, in meditation that was pain,
The city streets, and saw the thousand faces
Hurrying through that afternoon of rain—
All ages, all traditions, and all races—
Faces of beauty, faces like damned spirits,
Faces like leopards, faces like a stone—
Glimpses of all the human blood inherits.
And a beggar said: "May I speak to you alone?"
And on that rain-swept day I saw quite clear
That his mask was a replica of my own;
Behind his eyes hid the same secret fear
And bitter alienage I too had known.
And all the masks came suddenly crowding near,
Each one a beggar, terrified and alone.

XXIV

He who loves life, and has the winging thought
That rises into vistas of the air,
Views not his own fate with the blind despair
Of him who deems the whole world come to naught
In that hour when the little things he sought
No more shall be the treasures of his care,
And other lives shall his old passions wear,
And other dramas on this stage be wrought.
The great life-lover from his measured day,
Not separate from the mighty flow of things,
Looks out upon a far futurity—
And rising up on his strong spirit's wings
To view dim scenes a thousand years away,
Rejoices in a life that is not he.

XLV

And what is beauty? It is a going-home
To an adventure in an unknown land.
It is surprise that smites the spirit dumb,
Yet as familiar as a trusted hand.
It is a faring forth and a return—
A recognition where they glow apart
Of storm-blown lights whose lesser embers burn
Upon the hearthstone of the secret heart.
Beauty can be the reawakening spell
For wonders that the spirit always knew—
Or the strange coming of a miracle
That on the soul's dark threshold now proves true
As the heart sees, with dim incredulous eyes,
Itself the manger where a saviour lies.

L

In thousands toward the south the swallows fly:
They pause all morning here about my hill,
To veer and swoop and surge against the sky
Until their waves of multiple wing-beats fill
Half of the heavens:—foam-tossed like drops of spray
Aloft one moment—and then sweeping low
Down toward the fields in intricate changing play—
Then high once more—their rhythms weave and flow.
Such soaring of a thousand wills in one,
Such joy, such freedom, never have I known.
They are as leaves in some glad tempest blown,
Flashing and live beneath the autumn sun,
Revelling in a splendor of their own
Which by no dusk can ever be undone.

LII

For I have dreamed a dream where Fate and God
And all the words of wonder, blend to one

Immortal image:—that which from the sod
Arches unbroken to the farthest sun:
A rainbow for the unblindness of man's eyes
In those rare hours when with heroic faith
He sees, beyond his separate destinies,
A life so vast that it comprises death.
Then has he looked on nature. Not a good
Or evil but is pulse-beat of her heart.
Only the blindness of his finitude
Holds him dismayed, embittered, and apart—
Who might amid her vast mutations move,
Beyond the tyrannies of fear or love.

LIII

Mists on the mountain, mists far down the vale,
Everywhere dancers of the grey-eyed rain. . . .
A ghostly world, this day; and not in vain
I wandered forth to view its image pale.
The colored leaves in thousands now set sail
Down the great winds, and stark black boughs remain.
I see such beauty here as will not wane
But change to crystal in some winter gale.
The rocks are firm beneath my travelling foot.
High over hilltop, birds are circling south.
The mists, the mists, the endless mists go by.
Leafed on the vine hangs the dark ripening fruit. . . .
And sudden—there is set against my mouth
That wine which, tasted, slays mortality.

MIST

The mist came from an unknown place
And took the world away.
I woke at dawn to see my hills,
But all I saw was grey—

As limitless as time or space,
Vague as a maniac's dream.
The mist had borne my world away
On its insensate stream.

I turned my head and slept again—
Sleep is a sovereign art—
And when I woke, the hostile mist
Was blown, was strewn apart—

And I walked forth and saw my hills,
Trod them, and was content.
Yet still I dreamed a dream of mists
And what their coming meant.

I dreamed that in no lesser mist
The heart forever moves,
Seeing as vague ambiguous shapes
The forms it hates or loves—

And sees not clearly ever once
In this fog-haunted place
The actual sun, the actual hills,
Or the friend's actual face.

THE DEAD TREE

Bleak, bony-grey, its twisted branches rise
To stab in lightning-patterns at the skies.
Whatever else may die, it no more dies.

Triumphant and defiant there it stands;
Of Spring it makes no further brief demands;
It towers a monument above the lands.

It will return to that earth whence it came;
But now, a few years, like a frozen flame,
It spreads gigantic branches to proclaim

The swift dispersal of all life's distress
Whether the seasons smite or if they bless:—
The innocence of ultimate Nothingness.

SARA BARD FIELD

Sara Bard Field, of Los Gatos, California, is the widow
of the late Colonel Charles Erskine Scott Wood, whose
manuscripts, journals, diaries and correspondence she is now
organizing and annotating for the Huntington Library. She
has long been known as a poet in her own right, and has
published several collections of short verse and the long
poem *Barrabas*. She was born in Cincinnati, educated in
Detroit, lived for a time in Rangoon, Burma, and finally went
to Portland, Oregon, where she met and married Colonel
Wood. She has been active in the woman's suffrage crusade
and in other liberal and unifying movements.

COULD YOU NOT WATCH WITH ME
ONE LITTLE HOUR?

I am that woman who would wait the Dawn,
Nor slept while the slow moon rode into sight;
Who, fighting weariness, gazed full upon
The starry circle drawn about the night.
I saw the Milky Way fade like a cloud
And, drowsy-lidded, watched the distance grow
Between me and the Pleiades, nor bowed
To heavy hands of Sleep upon my brow.

Then, when night grew more stilly palpitate,
Listening for the faint birth-cry of morn,
And the cock crew, I, at the very gate,
Fell into cloddish slumber, all out-worn.
Even as I slept, soft as a look or sigh,
The Dawn with Love beside her passed me by.

I HAD A FAIR YOUNG SON

I had a fair young son but he is dead.
Lips wet with wormwood will not kiss the rood.
I found, instead, a granite bed—
The tomb of solitude
And sealed the wall so no one could intrude.

There I, a stone that lived to name the dead,
Heard weeping like a wind troubling space.
"Who broke the seal?" I cried. Their spokesmen said:
"The mothers were already in this place"—
And then I saw each shadow was a face.

"I had a fair young son but he is dead."
O lamentation old as motherhood!
How many mothers to the tomb have fled,
Even as I, alone with Death to brood,
Each finding she was with a multitude.

HE WHOM THE DEAD HAVE NOT FORGIVEN

I cry to the mountains; I cry to the sea.
I cry to the forest to cover me
From the terror of the invisible throng
With marching feet, the whole day long—
The whole night long,
Beating the accent of their wrong.

We whom the Dead have not forgiven
Must hear forever that ominous beat;

For the free, light, ripped air of heaven
Is burdened now with dead men's feet.

Feet that make solid the fluid space,
Feet that make weary the tireless wind,
Feet that leave grime on the moon's white face—
Black is the moon for us who have sinned!

And the mountains will not cover us,
Nor yet the forest nor the sea;
No storm of human restlessness
Can wake the tide or bend the tree.

Forever and ever until we die,
Through the once sweet air and the once blue sky
The thud of feet—the invisible throng,
Beating the accent of their wrong.

MAHLON LEONARD FISHER

Although his work has not been conspicuous during the past few years, Mahlon Leonard Fisher was known to all poetry lovers of a decade or two ago for his sonnets, some of which are as skillfully executed as any in the history of American literature. He was at one time editor of *The Sonnet*, now defunct. He was born on July 20, 1874, and is still living, at Williamsport, Pennsylvania.

IMMUTABILIS

The same blue sky, the same wide waste of sea,
The same green fields at even and at dawn,
The same swift-cycling seasons,—now the wan,
Weird pomp of Winter, now Spring's pageantry,—

That they of Eden knew, we know, and we,
As they, but watch the same white stars awake
From out their day-long lethargy and flake
The farthest arch of Dusk, unendingly.

And what was mystery then is mystery still!
Man has advanced but slowly: all his thought
Is vain beside one blosmy marvel wrought
Of seeming nothingness; the fern-fronds fill
His heart with wonder; and the tiniest blade
Of grass keeps its wee secret, unafraid!

TO A ROMAN DOLL

(Found in a Child's Grave in Hawara, Egypt)

What little Roman maiden loved you so?
Now, at the night, when one *I* love is led,
All drowsy-eyed and smiling, up to bed,
She holds her baby close—the way you know.
What little maiden was it, long ago,
Who pled for you before she fell asleep?
And did she dream of slumber centuries deep,
Where changeless dark should mask the morning's glow?
She held you all the ages on her breast.
What wondrous love was hers, outlasting thrones!
Her lullabies, outsounding battle tones,
Outlingering Iliads, brought unbroken rest.
Sphinx-like you gaze; but speak, lest Fame forget
Who waits you back in Egypt, faithful yet.

OF MELODIES UNHEARD

(To John Keats)

"Heard melodies are sweet, but those unheard
Are sweeter"?—then, O Poet of All Time,
How sweet it is with thee, where endless rhyme

More softly flows than faery-tides unstirred;
Where, all day long, no hint of half-spoke word,
However lyric, falls on listless ears,
And the hushed rains, more tenderly than tears,
Drip near the nest of some unvocal bird!

Yet all arch-harmonies are there, and thou,
Who knewest such, needs sense them in thy sleep,
And have sweet cognizance of seas where creep
The pristine Ships of Song, whose every prow
Doth cleave the Waves of Singing silence-crowned—
Lest some loud oar awake thee with a sound.

AFTERWARDS

There was a day when death to me meant tears,
And tearful takings-leave that had to be,
And awed embarkings on an unshored sea,
And sudden disarrangement of the years.
But now I know that nothing interferes
With the fixed forces when a tired man dies;
That death is only answerings and replies,
The chiming of a bell which no one hears,
The casual slanting of a half-spent sun,
The soft recessional of noise and coil,
The coveted something time nor age can spoil;
I know it is a fabric finely spun
Between the stars and dark; to seize and keep,
Such glad romances as we read in sleep.

HILDEGARDE FLANNER

The poems of Hildegarde Flanner have been known for
many years to discriminating readers of American poetry.

She is the author of several plays and a number of essays in addition to her magazine verse and her books, *Time's Profile* (Macmillan, 1929) and *If There Is Time* (New Directions, 1942). She was educated at the University of California, and lives at Altadena, in Southern California.

A WREATH FOR ASHES

I

Unsung, unsigned upon the dust of time,
　　Shall we sink down, we two, and sift together,
My song forgotten, and your lovely page
　　Blank in eternity's effacing weather?

Will the rain waver, and the vacant snow
　　Replace the beauty of a path we trod,
And the wind rustle and slip over us,
　　Lost between stars upon our way to God?

How tragic anger, then, how futile hate,
　　When two dazed atoms, wafted out of sight,
Vainly recall that such a thing as love
　　Existed this side of eternal night.

II

I am bereft of any word to utter.
　　Here on my lips no syllable is heard.
Look in my face—I have no word to give you.
　　Look in my eyes—I am widow to a word.

Of what avail to write a thousand poems
　　Or in love's history assume a part,
When every stroke of pen can only bury
　　Deeper the dead word in the sorrowing heart?

III

I know a wound that closes to the eye,
   Retreats from view and leaves no mark behind.
Sorrow has worn it smooth, but far beneath
   It sets a flaming circle on the mind.

There is a wound that disappears at last
   And one may say, "Observe that I am whole,"
But where no eye can see, no stranger guess,
   It bleeds indelibly upon the soul.

OTTO FREUND

Otto Freund was born in Springfield, Illinois; attended
Illinois College and New York University; and while still at
college began writing verse, both serious and humorous,
most of which appeared in various national magazines and
anthologies. He has also contributed humorous prose to the
Saturday Evening Post. For the past fifteen years he has
lived in Portland, Oregon.

The following selections illustrate not only his ability to
produce accomplished sonnets and lyrics, but his gift with
that small, many-faceted form, the quatrain.

THE ISLE OF THE DEAD

No sound is heard here where the grey cliffs rise
   From twilight-dreaming waters; no wind stirs
   Among the cypresses; dark harbingers
Of doom, the clouds drift low in sullen skies.
Within dim, glimmering gates the harbor lies
   Eternally aloof, hemmed in by spurs
   Of soaring granite; endless evening blurs
The placid depths with purple-gleaming dyes.

Too soon a spectral boatman, muffled, still,
  Breaks the long silence as with stealthy oar
    He dips the tranquil water, in his skiff
A passenger from some far, friendly hill
  Faring to join the pilgrims gone before—
    The dreamless sleepers under the dark cliff.

FOOTSTEPS

All day I hear them tapping in the street,
  The footsteps passing by;
Like castanets their quick crescendos beat,
  And quickly die.

On futile errands pressing to and fro
  Their echoes never cease;
In madness some, in sorrow others go,
  But none in peace.

Their owners blind, the misty goals they see
  Before them gleam and fade,
Like crumbling domes of wind-built fantasy,
  By winds decayed.

All day they go, the feet that never rest
  From fruitless, drab affairs,
Till night brings forth the stars, in silent quest
  As vain as theirs.

REQUIESCAT

John Barrymore

Unanswered encores, rue, and requiems sung,
  Forgetful dust, the turning of a page,
But still the voice of Hamlet rings among
  The silent galleries and an empty stage.

HEART WOUND

The wound is healed, but still the pain is there,
    And stabs with anguish, like a sudden sword,
When sunlight feigns the spun gold of her hair,
    Or music finds her lost voice in a chord.

MUSIC

Music can paint no pictures, speak no words,
    It has no visible hue, no formal motion,
But it can wing the heart to soar with birds,
    Transform the soul's self to a troubled ocean.

RALPH FRIEDRICH

Ralph Friedrich, who at this writing is engaged in a specialized study for the armed forces at Ann Arbor, Michigan, has contributed poems to the *Saturday Review of Literature, The American Mercury, New York Times,* and other periodicals. He has won several literary prizes, and is the author of one book, *Boy at Dusk.* Before his entry into the army, he taught English in the Cincinnati public schools.

EVEN ON A NIGHT LIKE THIS

Once upon a night like this,
Over Tyre and Babylon,
Over tranced Endymion,
Over dark Semiramis,

Over temples blooming white
From the shadowed hills of night,
Tides of moonlight poured and swept.

Cities shimmered as they slept
Sunken in a gulf of light.

Even on a night like this
Time was diligent, and grief.
Death, like any petty thief,
Coveted Diana's kiss.
In the rustle of a leaf

Menace spoke, and over Tyre,
Like foreshadowings of fire,
Moonbeams rippled. Babylon,
Moving eastward into dawn,
Mourned to know the night so brief.

Babylon is dust, and Tyre.
With a name, Semiramis
Combats death. Endymion
Wakes to no regretted dawn.
But upon a night like this

In the province of desire
Moon and shadow-play conspire,
And they glimmer, far and lost,
And the moonlight like a frost
Lies upon them. In a brief
Soundless moment they have crossed
Centuries to find their grief
Spoken by a trembling leaf.

GEORGIE STARBUCK GALBRAITH

Georgie Starbuck Galbraith was born in 1909, has lived
most of her life in California, and is a resident of Bakersfield

in that state. She began writing verse in 1938, and since 1942 her work has appeared in many poetry journals and in a number of popular magazines, including *Saturday Evening Post, Ladies' Home Journal, Good Housekeeping,* etc.

MIST

These thoughts of you, the memories and pain,
Do not come sudden like a blinding rain
Accompanied by the pulse-exciting crash
Of thunder, and the wild blue lightning's flash.
Ah no. The memories that chill and twist
My heart with torture come like autumn mist.
At first no more than shadow, just a hint
Of faint, suggested film, through which the glint
Of my inner sun still glows. Then fog-wraiths creep
Like phantoms rising out of opium sleep.
Insidious, intangible, they cloud
My consciousness, and weave a smothering shroud
To wrap about the brightness of my brain.
These thoughts of you do not descend like rain.
Subtly they come, and hauntingly persist,
Pervading, drifting, clinging . . . they are mist.

CLIFFORD GESSLER

Practically the whole of Clifford Gessler's life has been devoted to literary and journalistic activity. He was born at Milton Junction, Wisconsin, November 9, 1893; has engaged in newspaper work in Milwaukee, Indianapolis, Chicago and Honolulu; was literary editor of the *Star-Bulletin* in the latter city, 1924 to 1934; and since 1937 has been on the editorial staff of the *Oakland* (California) *Tribune*. He is known for several prose books on Mexico and the South

Pacific Islands as well as for his widely published verse; the latter, of which the latest collection is *Tropic Earth* (1944), is notable for its exotic atmosphere and for its portrayal of Polynesian life.

TIMELESS ISLAND

The hours reel off the golden spool of time
unmarked, here where no wheel has ever turned,
save by the slow, green changing of the tide,
the grave procession of the sun and stars.
Men rise, shake sleep from eyes and limbs, and go
to reap the day's food from the fruitful sea,
and women's fingers plait smooth mats of leaves,
and children skip the rope of twisted husks,
as velvet shadows glide across the sand.
Yet even here, the unregarded years
gnaw at the bud and branch and root—and men
ripen or wither, slowly, loosen hold
on the tree of life, and drop, as the withered leaf
or the ripened fruit, and the tide of change rolls on.
From time, even denied, there is no escape.

CHART OF THE PACIFIC

This paper flatness, yellow-isled, and neat
with parallel, meridian complete,
is not the Pacific. Here is not the sting
of blown spume hurtling in the face, the ring
of anchor-links against the chocks, the slosh
surging on tilted deck, the phosphor wash
streaming astern, or the small voice of bells
tinkling the sea's half hours, between the swells.
The sea is no dead thing of deftly drawn
latitudes, longitudes, but live as dawn
and cruel as absolute zero; it is kind

as food, and as indifferent as the stars
that weave cold-patterned webs between the spars.

THE FIRST POEM

Deftly he crashed the hammer tipped with stone
down on the brutish armor-plated skull;
his hairy arm drove swiftly with the dull
stone knife, until it bared the ponderous bone,
slashed to the cold slow heart—and with a groan
the great beast sank to earth. With one last pull
of saber claws it raked the victor full
across the fur-girt thighs, and hurled him prone.

And then as, battered, drenched with blood, and torn,
my far ancestor rose on wounded knees,
out of his throat a fierce bewildered cry
burst flaming forth, in rhythm that was borne
up through the shattered fronds of jungle trees:
thus man's first poem pierced the astonished sky.

GEORGIA B. GIERASCH

The poetry of Georgia B. Gierasch has sprung, as she de-
clares, out of "sheer and utter need of self-expression. Early
in life the violin sufficed and voice—later, the voice alone,
and then poetry." Mrs. Gierasch lives in New York City,
and since 1932 has published poems in more than a score of
verse magazines, and has written two book collections.

PANACEA

After day's persistent labor
From her closely curtained room
Comes a sound of ghostly rocking,

Rocking, rocking, ever rocking,
Rocking through the gloom.

Ingrid, are you always lonely,
Have you never ceased to mourn?
This the sound of ghostly rocking,
Rocking, rocking, ever rocking,
Every night reborn.

Never could she find an answer,
Hers a mind long gone astray;
But the sound of ghostly rocking,
Rocking, rocking, ever rocking,
Bears her far away.

Takes her to her faithless lover,
Brings the comfort of his arms;
And the echoes born of rocking,
Rocking, rocking, ghostly rocking,
Hold delusive charms.

LOUIS GINSBERG

Readers of modern poetry have frequently encountered the name of Louis Ginsberg in the pages of newspapers and magazines, and in anthologies edited by Rittenhouse, Moult, Untermeyer and others. A resident of Paterson, New Jersey, and a teacher of English for the past twenty years in one of its high schools, Mr. Ginsberg is the author of two volumes of verse. His work is characterized by its individuality, and frequently by its emotional and imaginative strength.

LETTER TO HEINE

You of the lyric, the ironic brow,
Heine, we need you now.
To flash the deathless sword of your bright song
Against the German wrong;
Help with your tender notes to solace well
Those fugitives from Hell.
Let your derision, let your scorn be poured
On Satan's brown-hued horde,
Tell them where faded Nineveh and Tyre
With rites of death and fire;
Those Pharaohs that once lifted haughty lids
Beside the pyramids;—
All Caesars, Genghis Khans, Napoleons,
All cruel, tyrannous ones!—
Tell how the worms were punctual once with these—
Summed their biographies!
How vain for men of the hour to flout with crime
The people of all time!
Embalm the burning of the books, the sham,
Within an epigram;
Impale all creatures that befoul their nest
Upon your glittering jest;
Those sadists over victims with their whips,
Prison in bitter quips;
All Torquemadas, turning back Time's clocks,
Trap in a paradox;
Instruct despoilers with your mocking pen
How Judah flowers again;
And to all murderers this mockery give:
How Death makes Judah live!
Heine, with lyric and ironic brow
We need you now!

LOST WORLD

Translucent in the flawless pond
   Like crystal-globe, inverted there,
A fringe of woods and sky beyond
   Are cleaned as by a purer air.

Here, freed from time, are sunk my dreams;
   My boyhood days lie anchored all;
Here, where a clear enchantment gleams,
   My youth is drowned beyond recall.

So, in its golden glory clad,
   The world I lost, I see it plain:
The happiness that once I had
   But that I cannot have again. . . .

MAE WINKLER GOODMAN

Mae Winkler Goodman passed her childhood on a Louisiana sugar plantation, moved in 1923 to Cleveland, where she still lives, and graduated from Western Reserve University in 1933. She has contributed numerous poems to magazines and newspapers, including nearly one hundred and forty to the *Cleveland Plain Dealer*.

AND WHO SHALL TELL?

And who shall tell the dreamer from the dream?
As interwoven as the day and night,
The dark receding as the day grows bright,
Or day withdrawing, leaving yet a gleam
Upon the earth—for ever must it seem
That they are one: the dreamer with his sight

Turned inward on the glow of some strange light,
The dream turned outward, part of that same scheme.

So clearly does it fit into His plan,
So perfectly are dream and dreamer wrought
That none need question, none need ask the way.
The dreamer He perfected,—that was man,—
His, too, the dream, to be forever sought,—
And they are one, even as night and day.

FRANCES ANGEVINE GRAY

Frances Angevine Gray is a graduate of the University of
Rochester, and teaches English in a Rochester high school.
She is the author of many magazine poems, as well as of one
book collection, *Fragile Armor*.

KALEIDOSCOPE

There is a toy called the kaleidoscope.
Before a child's charmed gaze it recombines
A hundred jeweled bits of colored glass
Into a myriad variant designs.

An instant's tremor brings a swift cascade,
A flood of azure, mauve, and crimson rivers.
Patterns disintegrate in swift descent,
If the young wrist or finger only quivers.

So burns this hour, amethyst, vert and amber,
Chance fragments poised in mortal symmetry,
Designed like dreams too radiant to remember,
Touched with ineffable, brief artistry.

Only too well I know how frail the pattern,
Fashioned of what cheap bits, how fleet to pass.
Against all reason, Life, do I beseech you,
Hold fast the cylinder, turn not the glass!

Arthur Guiterman

It was perhaps Arthur Guiterman's misfortune as a poet that he was celebrated for his facile light verse. For his mere chaff tended to obscure his capable and original serious poetry—poetry that in its upper reaches places him beside the best of his contemporaries. Possibly the fault was that he wrote too much; he published twenty books in all, of which fifteen were collections of verse; and more than four thousand of his poems have appeared in magazines and newspapers. Since he had a bent for light verse and found this to be what editors wanted, it is not surprising that he gave much of his effort to being the mere jester.

Guiterman was born in Vienna on November 20, 1871, of American parents; and passed most of his boyhood and much of his subsequent life in New York. He died on January 11, 1943, in Pittsburgh, while on the way to deliver a lecture on *Brave Laughter.*

NO KING

The locusts have no king, yet they go forth;
    They have no king, yet they go forth by bands;
The locusts have no king, yet South and North
    Their sullen armies desolate the lands.
Not Jenghiz Khan or Tamerlane the Great,
    Nor Alaric or Atilla the Hun
Ravaged like these; no wall or brazen gate
    Delays their march; their clouds blot out the sun,

Their wings roar like the sea, their evil jaws
  Champ, champ unceasingly; and where their vast,
Ungoverned hordes, whose hunger finds no pause,
  Have made their bivouac, have come and passed,
No leaf, flower, fruit of any growing thing
  Of earth remains. And yet—they have no king!

THE METEORITE

Was this the flaming thunderbolt of Jove
  That crushed the last of earth's gigantic race—
  Some frenzied Titan battling to efface
The might that made him? What is he that strove
Against Omnipotence? What engine drove
  Through silent leagues of unimagined space
  These ragged tons that passed and left no trace
But cloven mountain-side, or blasted grove?

What daring mind may dream of what you are,
  O vagrant flake of heaven's iron showers
    That fall, forever fall, on land or sea?
Sky derelict, rude wreckage of a star,
  Stern evidence of other worlds than ours,
    Grim sign that greater worlds have ceased to be!

DORA HAGEMEYER

Dora Hagemeyer, who runs a poetry column in the Carmel (California) *Pine Cone*, has published numbers of magazine poems in addition to *The Shining Wind* (1944), a privately issued collection of her verses. She was born in Gawler, South Australia; passed most of her childhood in New Zealand; and in 1915 came to California, her home ever since.

IN THE PASTURE

Tired, tired of soul she walked across the field
Away from war-news, grieving for mankind . . .
Seeing no way of promise that could yield
Hope for the future—disillusioned—blind—
Walking for sorrow's sake and that alone,
Her heart the chill grey numbness of the stone.

Having no aim but aimlessness she leaned
Against the fence, dull-staring into space . . .
There came a little colt, oh barely weaned,
On shaky legs, and looked into her face,
Staring into her soul with great dark eyes
Open and wide, too artless for surprise.

She looked into those depths of innocence,
Those wide deep wells of trust, so morning-clear—
Too full of love to hide the least pretense,
So pure, so utterly devoid of fear,
And gazed and gazed until her grieving soul
Was somehow gathered homeward and made whole.

THE CHOICE

Two angels stood with dawn beside my bed,
One bearing joy—the very topmost fruit;
The other pain, the bitter draught new-bled
From the same tree, but from the deepest root;

Two equal angels offering me their gifts—
And I bewildered, blind as from the sun,
Reach forth for both. The veil of vision lifts,
And lo, within my hand the two are one!

Amanda Benjamin Hall

Amanda Benjamin Hall (Mrs. John A. Brownell) is known as the author of four books of verse as well as of several prose volumes. She has won prizes from the Poetry Society of America, *Poetry* of Chicago, and other sources; and has been published time after time in leading anthologies as well as in periodicals. She was born in Hallville, Connecticut, on July 12, 1890, and has lived for many years in New London in the same state.

BOY FOURTEEN

As he goes whistling down his fourteenth year,
Imbued with secret purpose like a cloud,
No belted earl nor lofty cavalier
Was ever half so arrogant. . . . That proud
Reserve of his can wound like David's sling
If he perceive himself too closely pressed
By humans, yet the least bird that wears wing
Or creature furred, he'll make his honored guest.
Then mark how courteous he is to crows,
To garter snakes or frogs in gaudy vesture,
And how at night-time, snug in bed, he throws
The covers back and, with a cordial gesture,
Invites the mongrel pup therein to dream
As token of his favor and esteem.

THE STRANGER

I ask myself forever, "Who am I?"
Finding at night my hair is still awake
Upon the frosty pillow. Breezes make
A dark plague of its tendrils as they fly.
And strange as death, and white as silver lie
My alien arms beside me. . . . All unnamed,

The soul hides in its little house, ashamed
To come without credentials from the sky.

But when the day redeems its promise, when
The gray and lilac pigeons tread the gold
Of some tall turret or illustrious shelf,
And women, bright as goddesses, and men
Step from their doors, I greet the human mold,
And like an orphan child I name myself

MAURINE HALLIBURTON

The following poem was contributed several years ago to an American magazine by Mrs. M. H. McGee, who lived in Tulsa, Oklahoma, and wrote under the pen-name of Maurine Halliburton.

INCARNATION

They saw her standing in the field
Where they had seen but rows of wheat,
Her beauty was a blazing shield
Their eyes could scarcely meet.

The harvesters who saw her say
There was a glory where she stood:
The wheat in gilded hummocks lay,
The stubble silver to the wood.

And all about the scene was fair—
As if by magic touch, the same
Familiar fields, the sunny air,
Were like a picture in a dream.

Then she was gone; but if she walked
Or ran or vanished with the light
They did not know, and wildly talked
Among themselves until the night.

She never came that way again
Nor ever in the wood was seen,
But still the harvesters explain
Her beauty and her gracious mien.

A little while one day, of all
The days the wheat was harvested,
She stood among it to enthrall
Their sight, transcending toil and bread,

That ever after they might tell
Of beauty far beyond their ken,
And how a glory round her fell
Upon the startled harvestmen.

ELOISE HAMILTON

Eloise Hamilton is a native Californian, long since transplanted to her present home in Portland, Oregon. She was the organizer and first president of the Portland poetry society, the "Verseweavers," and has been active in various other literary groups. Aside from her verse, she has done much news reporting, and has written a number of special articles for newspapers and magazines.

THE WEAVER

The quiet Persian seated at her loom
With patterned beauty at her finger-tips,

Has lost the freshness of her early bloom,
And stilled the longing of her eager lips.

With patterned beauty at her finger-tips
She sees a Master-plan take shape and grow;
Between her flying hands the shuttle slips,
Responsively the vibrant colors glow.

She sees a Master-plan take shape and grow—
A pattern traced upon no formal chart;
Only the worker and the master know
The figures graven on a weaver's heart!

A pattern traced upon no formal chart,
But day by day remembered, slowly laid
Across a timeless warp—a living part
Of a predestined blend of light and shade.

Long day by day remembered, slowly laid
In rich mosaic. The weaver is resigned
That life became this perfect thing she made,
Her twisted hands lie still—she has grown blind!

You see exquisite beauty in my room?
I see a quiet Persian at a loom!

MARION ETHEL HAMILTON

A contributor to many magazines and the author of three volumes of verse, of which the latest is *The Ultimate Lover*, Marion Ethel Hamilton is a resident of San Diego, California. She has attained considerable proficiency as a writer both of lyrics and of sonnets, examples of her work in both forms being given below.

GAUGUIN

Within his hut he lay at flaming noon;
And time was not, for him, and conscience dead;
Only the purple seas beating their rune,
And walls all splashed with pictures, yellow and red.
And a great passion brooding in his face,
And a great passion burning in his blood,
To catch the essence of this primitive race
Before it was swept on, as by a flood.
And here he worked and dreamed, and here despaired,
And drew his dusky figures, innocent-eyed;
His world in Paris thought he had not cared,
And yet—they found these pictures, when he died—
A Breton village, huddled under snow,
And his two children, whom he did not know.

RACHEL LAMENTS

O Rachel, crying and lamenting loud,
For children that you crave, and who are not—
The shadowy centuries are long forgot,
But I am bowed with woe, as you were bowed.
We are the childless mothers, not allowed
To hold our own, although our hearts are hot
With bitterness, and hatred of our lot.
And we must look on women who are proud.

It is our fate to be misunderstood;
Our hearts lamenting, but our heads held high,
Wearing a crown of beauty, or of fame;
When for that ancient crown of motherhood,
We might have given life without a sigh,
Gone gladly blinded, or forever lame.

DREAM

What is this dream I have, between sleeping and waking?—
This dream of walking the English moors in the twilight?
I, who never have stepped a foot upon England,
Walking the purple moors in the windy twilight.

What is this dream I have, between sleeping and waking?—
Of walking a road alone, and coming from darkness
Into the light of a camp; the firelight on evil faces—
Strangeness and fear, then diving again into darkness?

What is this dream called life, between sleeping and sleep-
    ing?
This coming from darkness to light, non-being to being?
Life is a gipsy camp . . . a light upon evil faces. . . .
Death is darkness again, and windy moors in the twilight.

Ruth Guthrie Harding

Ruth Guthrie Harding, widow of the noted poet and lecturer Richard Burton, has long been known as a poet in her own right. She has published one book, *A Lark Went Singing*, and has been in a number of the standard anthologies; her work is remarkable not only for its insight and its emotional undertones but for its rhythmical sensitiveness. She is at present busy on an autobiographical work soon to be published. Born in Tunkhannock, Pennsylvania, on August 20, 1882, she lives today in Ridgewood, New Jersey.

NIGHT PULSE

I press my ear to my pillow as a child his ear to a shell,
My eyelids close with the drifting of fragments of vanished
    years:

Shadow instead of substance—and sound of a harbor bell—
This is the pattern of heart-beats, the measure of unshed
    tears.
Fires that burned to ashes, young rapture that could not
    stay,
Moments of labor and sorrow, moments of laughter and
    light,
Faces of friends remembered and voices from yesterday:
Of these does the shell of silence make tides in the autumn
    night . . .
Of these does the moving shuttle weave cloth-of-sleep too
    thin
For warming the lonely darkness or hiding what is to be.
I to whom Time brings vision know well that my shores
    begin
To fade on the last horizon at meeting of river and sea.

.   .   .   .   .

Wrists throb with an upland meadow
Where the Susquehanna curves . . .
Bowman's Creek in the springtime
And path that dips and swerves . . .
Laurel and mandrake thicket
And wild grape's twisted rope . . .
The gray of cold North Mountain
Seen from the Crestmont slope.

.   .   .   .

Poets are dead who told us that rhythm is breath of song,
But out from their folded pages comes grace that used to be
And stirs a memoried music from strings forsworn too long—
("Uprose the sun," says my pillow, "and uprose Emily" . . .)
Spanish sailors in Portland; a barge on a twilit stream
And Lancelot's pity glimpsing the lost name on the prow;
Marshes of Glynn wide-reaching to ledges of lyric dream;
Beauty in ancient rhyming of Helen's tender brow.

.   .   .   .

Surges within my temples
The arc of Monhegan Light . . .
Gleam of Nevada desert . . .
Mount Rose's granite height . . .
Rain and moonlight blending
On hedges at Punahou . .
Sands of Florida beaches
Stretching to boundless blue.

. . . .

I press my ear to my pillow as a child his ear to a shell,
My eyelids close with my holding of broken bits of the past:
Shadow rather than substance—and sound of a sunken bell—
This will be pattern of heart-beats for me at the quiet last.

ON A FLY-LEAF OF SCHOPENHAUER'S
IMMORTALITY

There is nothing new to be written of tears and man's shud-
    dering breath;
Nothing new to be said of his loving, or sinning, or death;
Nothing new to be thought of his loneliness under the sky—
But something is new in the knowledge that soon it will have
    to be I
Who will give over weeping and breathing, relinquish my
    love and my load,
And lie in the dark and the quiet that waits at the end of
    the road.

* * *

There is nothing new to be whispered of blossoms breaking
    the sod,
But something is new in my asking—*"Take care of me, God!"*

VALSE TRISTE
(Sibelius)

Slow strings are vibrant in the first deep note:
I know too well the time I heard them last,

And feel the blocked pulse throbbing in my throat.
I clasp tense hands against the whispering past
And close hot eyes against a memoried face
Lest I drop tears that must not here be shed.
I sit with strangers in an alien place. . . .
Waiting six beats to bring me back my dead.
Too brief the flaming of that poignant spark
Of tender sound: how quickly it is gone!
Ashes of music lie upon the dark
Of other phrases as they follow on.
In brave, proud quiet and with head held high
I dare the glances that may chance to rest
On my still brow. None listening hears the sigh
Through the last cadence . . . breathed against my breast.

PEACE IS ONLY AN INTERLUDE

Beyond the guns in Libya the Roman trumpets sound
And Caesar's legions camp tonight near many a battle-
    ground;
The tides of storied oceans rise and whisper to the stars
Of ships with rows of galley-slaves and oddly fashioned
    spars.

The planes that drop their fiery load from out an alien sky
Have Kentish bowmen in the pits, and arrows whistle by;
Ghost-figures with the ark ahead move silent to and fro,
And they that lead the stalwart host fought once at Jericho.

We add but single chapters to a tale that never ends,
We offer only drama that with ageless drama blends,
And Man with Man contending for the glory and the power
Could read his vengeant passing in a strident summer
    shower . . .

Could know his gathered holdings for a field of ripened grain
Made ready for the sickles of some thieving gypsy-train,

Could learn his future nothingness from troubadours and
 bards
Who sang of mighty fortresses that now are crumbling
 shards.

Cassandra on the battlements still makes her deathless croon
And lifts her weirdly supple hands to stay the drifting moon:
Behind the lines of muddy tanks that cross the Russian fields,
King Priam's armies in the dusk are braced against their
 shields.

ELIZABETH STANTON HARDY

Elizabeth Stanton Hardy was born in Cleveland, Ohio,
but after her marriage she moved to Rochester, New York,
where she has taught poetry technique in the University of
Rochester, and elsewhere. Her book of verse, *Time in the
Turning*, was published in 1940. She is a contributor to the
poetry magazines.

SEA SHELL

Out from this fluted shell the muffled roar
Murmurs monotonously to the ear—
Seas that have dashed on some Archaean shore
Now whisper to a hollow hemisphere;

And even we, who have so lately come
Upon the sands of an eternal sea,
Hold echoes of a past millennium
Sounding the drift of immortality.

AMORY HARE

The work of Amory Hare has appeared in the *Atlantic,
Harper's, Harper's Bazaar, Cosmopolitan,* and other maga-
zines; her books of verse have borne the imprint of Macmil-
lan, Dodd, Mead, and John Lane; a novel was published some
time ago by Scribner. She was born in Philadelphia in 1885,
and until recently lived at Media, Pennsylvania, but is at
present a resident of Santa Ynez, California. Her poems,
notable for their lyrical qualities, have been known for years.

AFTER

One with the ploughed field,
One with the lark's flight,
One with the wheat's yield,
One with the night;

Swift in the sea-spray
Where the snipe hurry,
Quick in the Spring's way
When buds are furry;

Part of the root's urge
Groping below,
And of the wind's surge
Where the leaves blow;

Strong in the new grass
When the wind shakes it
Where the slow herds pass
Or the scythe takes it—

I shall be near to thee
Eager for sharing

Far though the voyage be,
Long be the faring.

Thou who art dear to me
Years go so fast!
Thou shalt come here to me
And be, at last,

One with the ploughed field,
One with the lark's flight,
One with the wheat's yield,
One with the night.

ECHO

I think when you have ridden toward the sun
Some golden dusk, forgetting to return,
These dawns that dream, these evening skies that burn,
These hills where we have watched the quiet hours
Painting the changeling seasons, one by one;
These dim woods with their drift of dogwood flowers
Will bring me news of you, and I shall come
For comradeship to these old hills of home.

It may have been for this that I have heard
The language of the night, the speech of trees,
The brown brook busy with old melodies,
The wood dove's repetition of a word
Whose meaning Time has filched from Summer's purse;
It may be but for this that I rehearse
The brimming hours before the light is gone
And one of us is bidden to ride on.

TO A LITTLE GIRL

Here in this darkened room, as daylight goes,
I bend above the sheltered little bed,

And watch the outline of the small dark head,
Touched with the beauty of a child's repose.
Dim little soul! what wonder yet to be!
Frail body, what a miracle your part!
Pray God the one who comes to claim your heart
Be worthy of your pain and ecstasy.
Strange that these tiny hands shall tend one day
Another, who shall know the earth through you;
Strange that these lips, that sorrow never knew,
Shall, one day, teach another soul to pray!

DONALD WING HATHAWAY

Donald Wing Hathaway, a graduate of Northwestern University, lives in Evanston, Illinois, where he works at his chosen occupation as a teacher of the blind. His poems have appeared in a number of the verse magazines.

ETCHERS OF ELD

Over a crystal table
    Gravely at work they lean—
Gray men of wrinkled faces,
    Eyes that are clear and clean.

Long they bend at their labor,
    Etching under a lens,
Over silvery paper
    Moving silvery pens.

They gloss and glaze, they embellish
    With feather and barb and bar
(Fretted out of frost-foil)
    Many a million star,—

While around the glittering table
Winds unwearied go
In their cloudy hair forever
Gathering the snow.

KATHARINE SHEPARD HAYDEN

Katharine Shepard Hayden is the author of *Sonnets and Lyrics* (1934) and of poems that have appeared in the *Saturday Evening Post, Scribner's, New York Times,* and many other periodicals.

FROM THE CLIFFS AT PUYE, NEW MEXICO

This is the dewy morning of the world—
All the wide earth, the mountains, fold on fold,
Lie azure on the pure horizon furled;
Here, like a mellow rim of ancient gold
Above the pines, scoured by the sun and rains,
Far from the desert canyons and the trails
That lead to watered valleys and the plains,
The cliffs are set. Never a bird that sails
These upper skies is more instinct with peace
Than this forgotten bastion where the air
Brings the dulled sense and spirit soft release
From cluttered weariness till all lies bare,
Unstained magnificence of being lies
As clear and still as earth before my eyes.

AFTER A SYMPHONY CONCERT

Who would have dreamed, hearing the wind at night
In the first forest of the world, **that men**
Could capture it like this for their delight—

Leading it out through flutes and horns? And when
The flight of arrows left the hunter's bow
Twanging within his grasp, who dreamed the thin
Fainting vibration should through ages grow
Into the rapture of the violin?
That ever, with their curious instruments,
Men, who are else but mute in woe and bliss,
Would break beyond the farthest firmaments
Of spirit and of sky, with speech like this?
Building of wingèd tones such symphonies
The very spheres must cry, "What gods are these!"

JESSIE M. HEINER

Jessie M. Heiner, a graduate of Ohio State University and
resident of Columbus, Ohio, is a regular contributor to the
Columbus Dispatch, under the pen-name of Margarethe
McCrae. She has lectured, written short stories, and con-
tributed to leading newspapers and poetry magazines; and
is the author of one volume, *Beckoning Paths*, issued in 1944.

THE MASK

Love fled that bitter house one day,
Nor Laughter tarried long;
And Music gathered up her notes,
Save one poor haunting song.

Love never stopped to look behind,
And Laughter, too, was mute;
But Music hummed a somber tune
Of shining dead-sea fruit.

Yet still to that strange bitter house,
Guests came and broke the bread,

And sipped the wine—nor seemed to know
The living were the dead.

DuBose Heyward

Few if any writers of recent times have portrayed the
South and its people with more graphic power and fidelity
than has DuBose Heyward, who is perhaps best known for
his *Porgy*, a novel which in its dramatized form was an out-
standing Broadway success. But Heyward was also a poet,
and one capable of a searing reality of utterance; he pub-
lished three volumes of verse, one in collaboration with
Hervey Allen; and in these the Negroes and the white moun-
tineers are depicted with strokes of a rare incisiveness.

Heyward was born in Charleston, South Carolina, August
31, 1885, and remained closely associated with the South
until his death on July 16, 1940.

THE MOUNTAIN GIRL

Life ripens swiftly in these lonely hills,
Ripens, then hangs long-withered on the bough.
Out of their ancient hates, relentless wills,
And unsaid loves, youth burgeons fierce and strong,
Ready for life when life has scarce begun;
Eager to spend its all and then be done.

So, as I gaze at Dorothea now,
Wind-blown against the cabin's weathered side,
Defiant, flushed, with bodice blowing wide,
And rain-soaked homespun skirt that cannot hide
The bold, strong, ardent curves of womanhood;
My exultation winces into pain.

Youth, splendid, careless, racing with the rain,
Laughing against the storm as it shouts by.
And yet, perhaps when I pass here again,
Hid from the heat of weathers, she will be
One of the sunken, burned-out lives I see
Here where the mountains shoulder to the sky.

So, as the storm goes smashing down the range,
Striking white fire from the smitten hills,
Swelling the falls and streams until it fills
The cove with giant's music, wild and strange,
The laugh she sends across the shaken air
Brings sudden tears; its very triumph sings
Of beauty so intense it cannot last
Beyond the transient day of fragile things
That brush us, like a wind from unseen wings,
And then are gathered up into the past.

THE MOUNTAIN WOMAN

Among the sullen peaks she stood at bay
And paid life's hard account from her small store.
Knowing the code of mountain wives, she bore
The burden of the days without a sigh;
And, sharp against the somber winter sky,
I saw her drive her steers afield each day.

Hers was the hand that sunk the furrows deep
Across the rocky, grudging southern slope.
At first youth left her face, and later, hope;
Yet through each mocking spring and barren fall,
She reared her lusty brood, and gave them all
That gladder wives and mothers love to keep.

And when the sheriff shot her eldest son
Beside his still, so well she knew her part,

She gave no healing tears to ease her heart;
But took the blow upstanding, with her eyes
As drear and bitter as the winter skies.
Seeing her then, I thought that she had won.

But yesterday her man returned too soon
And found her tending, with a reverent touch,
One scarlet bloom; and, having drunk too much,
He snatched its flame and quenched it in the dirt.
Then, like a creature with a mortal hurt,
She fell, and wept away the afternoon.

EPITAPH OF A POET

Here lies a spendthrift who believed
That only those who spend may keep;
Who scattered seeds, yet never grieved
Because a stranger came to reap;

A failure who might well have risen;
Yet, ragged, sang exultantly
That all success is but a prison,
And only those who fail are free;

Who took what little Earth had given,
And watched it blaze, and watched it die;
Who could not see a distant Heaven
Because of dazzling nearer sky;

Who never flinched till Earth had taken
The most of him back home again,
And the last silences were shaken
With songs too lovely for his pen.

DANIEL WHITEHEAD HICKY

Daniel Whitehead Hicky sprang into prominence in the early Thirties, and was until recently one of the most widely published of American poets. His typical vein is a lush lyricism which, if at times lacking in depth, is almost invariably authentic poetry. His home is in Atlanta, Georgia.

MACHINES

I hear them grinding, grinding through the night,
The gaunt machines with arteries of fire,
Muscled with iron, bowelled with smouldering light;
I watch them pulsing, swinging, climbing higher,
Derrick on derrick, wheel on rhythmic wheel,
Swift band on whirring band, lever on lever,
Shouting their songs in raucous notes of steel,
Blinding a village with light, damming a river.
I hear them grinding, grinding, hour on hour,
Cleaving the night in twain, shattering the dark
With all the rasping torrents of their power,
Groaning and belching spark on crimson spark.
I cannot hear my voice above their cry
Shaking the earth and thundering to the sky.

Slowly the dawn comes up. No motors stir
The brightening hill-tops as the sunrise flows
In yellow tides where daybreak's lavender
Clings to a waiting valley. No derrick throws
The sun into the heavens and no pulley
Unfolds the wildflowers thirsting for the day;
No wheel unravels ferns deep in a gulley;
No engine starts the brook upon its way.
The butterflies drift idly, wing to wing,
Knowing no measured rhythm they must follow;

No turbine drives the white clouds as they swing
Across the cool blue meadows of the swallow.
With all the feathered silence of a swan
They whirr and beat—the engines of the dawn.

ROBERT HILLYER

Robert Hillyer, Pulitzer Prize winner in poetry for 1934
and author of many books of verse and criticism, was born
in East Orange, New Jersey, in 1895; and, following his grad-
uation from Harvard in 1917, saw service abroad for two
years as an ambulance driver with the American Expedi-
tionary Forces. In 1920-21 he studied in Copenhagen as a
fellow of the American-Scandinavian Foundation; and upon
his return to America began teaching at Harvard, where from
1937 until his resignation early in 1945 he was Boylston Pro-
fessor of Rhetoric and Oratory. His work, while perhaps not
so sharply individualized nor so striking in context as that of
many of his contemporaries, is marked throughout by a
classic gravity and finish.

SONNET

He who in spring's rebirth has put his trust
Now answers not to April nor to May,
Nor sees the moon-white apple blossoms sway,
Nor breathes its sweetness on the evening gust.
He who was first to climb the heights of day
Lies full-length in the valley of the dust;
His sword sleeps in his hand, and it is rust;
His heart sleeps in his breast, and it is clay.

Brother, so mute among the fallen years,
We come at dayspring to your living tomb

That is the green earth, and we shed no tears,
Knowing that if you wander otherwhere
Soon will you give us gracious welcome there,
And if you perished, then we share your doom.

THE CURTAINS DRAW ACROSS THE BRAIN

The curtains draw across the brain
And in that lighted house of mirth,
Secure from all the eyes of earth,
Our troupe of dreams come out again.

Folly has donned the sage's mask,
Wisdom appears the Knave of Hearts,
Yet in these topsy-turvy parts
They seem as real as one could ask;

As real as when they change their rôles
To be themselves and haunt the dream
Where for some hours of day they seem
Important to our sleeping souls.

FROM THE FOOTHILLS

By many paths we reach the single goal,
And all our quarrels deal but with its name;
There is no soul so different from my soul
As in its essence to be not the same.
No warrior but in his heart must know
How triumph is not proud nor vengeance sweet,
For he beholds, who slays the kindred foe,
Himself, self-murdered, lying at his feet.
It has been written that we are the islands
Which, ocean-sundered into seeming twain,
Are truly of one continent, the highlands
Wrought of one rock and rooted in one plain.
Bright Himalayan peace! the humblest crest
One with the splendour of Mount Everest.

THE MIRRORS OF ALL AGES

The mirrors of all ages are the eyes
Of some remembering god, wherein are sealed
The beauties of the world, the April field,
Young faces, blowing hair, and autumn skies.
The mirrors of the world shall break, and yield
To life again what never really dies;
The forms and colors of earth's pageantries
Unwithered and undimmed shall be revealed.
And in that moment silence shall unfold
Forgotten songs that she has held interred,
The ocean rising on the shores of gold,
Flecked with white laughter and love's lyric word;
All happy music that the world has heard;
All beauty that eternal eyes behold.

SOPHIE HIMMELL

Sophie Himmell, the author of one book. *Within the Crucible,* is a resident of New York City. Her poems, which have appeared in numerous publications, are characterized by an occasional epigrammatic turn, and by an incisive individual quality of penetration.

THE PAIN OF STONE

Let those who will on science meditate,
The lords of logic, masters of the knife;
Let them with naked candor find a life
In stone, and let them trace the trenchant date
Of their discovery upon the heart—
Into the living deathlessness of lime;
And let them mark each bleeding vein of time:
Such is their livelihood and such their art.

I need no bladed tool for finding truth,
Nor aid of logic's stern indifference:
I heard, when I was but a callow youth,
A thunder-riven boulder's piteous groan—
With feeling of profoundest reverence,
Though I was young, I knew the pain of stone.

THOUGH YOUR WORDS BE MESSENGERS OF HATE

Our thoughts are torpid as an ice-locked stream;
Shrouded in apathy they lie as dead,
While gargoyle phantoms of a troubled dream
Embrace in granite grasp our marriage bed.
Among the stalking shadows silence waits
To leap upon us like a cornered beast;
Dark centuries of mutely brooding hates
Make desolation of our copious feast.

What brute ancestral spirit's curse is this—
What incantation of an evil spell?
What demon witness of our nuptial kiss
In laughing rage has hurled us to this hell?
Speak, for tomorrow fumbles at the gate:
Speak, though your words be messengers of hate.

UNLESS I LEARN TO WALK UPRIGHT

Unless I learn to walk upright
Facing the javelins of scorn,
To seek no safeguard from the thrust
Of mockery's swift, sudden horn;
Unless I learn to sleep with pain,
Unshrinking from her spear-scarred side,
Why was I given at my birth
The noble heritage of pride?

Dorothy Hobson

Dorothy Hobson's poems began to appear in magazines about fifteen years ago, and in 1933 she published her first book, *Celestial Interim*. In 1936 she founded that significant institution which she terms "the now modestly successful" League to Support Poetry, and has been its volunteer director and hardest worker ever since. Her output in recent years has been slim because of this time-consuming effort on behalf of other poets, but her second volume, *Let There Be Light*, was published in the fall of 1943. In private life she is Mrs. Alfred Fitzgerald.

MEDITATION
1942

Let our smooth modern laughter still deride,
O brothers, if it can, the thought of sin;
Let the real shape of Satan be denied,
Now that we've seen him straddle Earth, a grin
Stretching his mouth, and seen God crucified
Ten million times upon ten million trees
(Blows rained on Him, if on the least of these . . .)

Watching that fierce embodiment of doom—
The hunter, nightmare-large, pursuing man
With hounds of famine, torture, anguish—loom
Within our gates, let anyone who can
Avoid the mirror; fail to recognize
Who helped to bloat that shape to giant-size.
Let him refute the likeness of that vast
And evil visage to his very own
As it was often in the careless past,
When greedily he thought of self alone,
Forgot his fellow-man, creating sin—

Dark aid for Lucifer that seemed unreal
Till its world-total was projected in
Misguided armies hurling fire and steel . . .

Let him who will, ignore the seeds that yield
This growth of horror; I myself cannot:
This bitterest war is one that must be fought
In mind and heart as on the battlefield:
The soul, too, has its fox-holes of Bataan,
Its jungles where self-treachery must be caught,
Its zero-cold of loneliness, its hot
Deserts of hate, its weary seas to span,
And breathless mountains to be climbed, defended
Till this long warfare of the God in man
Against the devil in him shall be ended.

MAN RETURNS TO THE GATES OF EDEN

Now we are suddenly afraid,
O angel with the burning sword;
This chaos is not what we meant
When first we confidently played
With knowledge; loving what the Lord
Had shaped, we copied mountains, sent
Each stone crag soaring further toward
The heavens, made our evenings blaze
Whiter, more brilliant than the days
With simulated sun, stars, moon;
With mighty dams, we fashioned lakes . . .
We must have tried to spell too soon
Like the child-prodigy who plays
Sonatas flatly as a scale,
Or somehow we have made mistakes
Like the seer's apprentice in the tale.

Now thunder and lightning shake the towers,
Dimmed are the luminous colored shams

We decked our nights with, and the dams
Are broken, while the darkling powers
We summoned in our early pride
At imitating gods, now ride
Over us, and our human blood
Spills out into the hoof-whipped mud.

Now we are terribly afraid;
We did not mean this, when we played
At copying as best we could
The mountain-peak, the sea, the sun;
What did we leave unsaid, undone?
Was love, perhaps, was brotherhood,
Essential word we knew so well,
Omitted when we said the spell?

Though you cannot let us in again,
Be lenient to us in our pain:
Speak, tell us the forgotten word,
O angel with the burning sword.

ALMA ELLIS HOERNECKE

Alma Ellis Hoernecke was born in Tidewater, Virginia, and was educated in several old southern colleges, at two of which she subsequently taught English, French and German; later, she studied Medieval French in Paris, and did much writing under private tutors. Since her marriage, she has lived at her country home near Vienna, Maryland. She is the author of numbers of unusually feeling and sensitive magazine poems.

TO ME AND NOT TO THEM

Unhearing all, who would have loved my song:
The clever one whose quick, tart tongue belied
The self-renouncing that she willed to hide;
The jovial one, the tender, weak and strong;
The one far-thinking to whom should belong
These small brain children she would not deride;
The friend I thought no evil could betide;
To me and not to them Death did the wrong.

The ironic years grant joy that holds a fear,
The fear we hide while joy is on the lip.
What is so closely held is none the less
What least we own. And then comes emptiness.
Who should have drained her cup dared still to sip—
They, they are gone and I alone am here!

HE HAS FINE EYES

He has fine eyes! Ah, think how much that means
In human meagreness. Hunchbacked or lame,
The eyes have power to hide the body's shame—
The eyes that are the spirit's poorest screens;
Through them men peer, uncaught, behind the scenes
Where thoughts put on and off their wigs at will,
And dress for rôles they'll play for good or ill,
As beggars, princes, poets, hags or queens.

Then when death comes, these doors are closed to hide
The emptiness within. What dwelt there fled.
The tent that housed a man could not abide,
But where is that because of which we said:
"He has fine eyes"? Gone far, we know not where;
We only know that now nothing is there.

Homer C. House

Although he began writing poetry late in life, a rare and varied talent was manifested by Dr. Homer C. House, head of the English Department at the University of Maryland, and founder of the Authorship Club at College Park. Humor, satire and serious work appeared from his pen in a continuous stream for a number of years, was published abundantly in periodicals throughout the country, and was assembled in two volumes, *Sun Dance* and *The Shadow of a Man*. Dr. House died suddenly on August 28, 1938, while on a lecture tour to the Pacific Coast.

VOICES

All else shall die; voices alone live on.
   The midnight surge of ocean falls away
And sinks to lonely stillness while the dawn
   Is heralding the fair and quiet day.

Voices alone live on; all else shall die.
   The hugest armament—its banners furled,
Its vast and murder-belching guns shall lie
   And rot as carrion strewn about the world.

Voices alone, or low, or high in song,
   Alert in human brain or poet's page,
Shall challenge death and all his serried throng,
   In everlasting youth, in deathless age.

Here the firm earth our hope must stand upon
(All else shall die)—voices live on and on.

INSOLENCE

Man's hour is such a puny thing and slight—
A tale that ends ere it is well begun,
A point of fire against a wall of night,
A mote that flickers in the setting sun!

The mountains and the sea are his despair:
He with his racing hopes like beating wings;
They with their nonchalant, immobile air,
The stolid, cruel front of lifeless things.

In terror he invents a Larger Man,
And older far than sea or continent,
Outlasting any stream that ever ran,
And in His own eternity content.

But when illusion leaves the troubled brain
And fancy grows reality at last,
Once more he looks from out his house of pain
Upon the ancient mountains, grim and vast.

He must endure (oh, worst of human ills),
His helpless fingers gripping brutal bars,
The supercilious patience of the hills,
The rapt, insulting quiet of the stars.

HOME

Upon the shadowy sunset bound of sleep
    My feet a moment quite forgot to roam—
A slanting beam across the darkening deep
    Picked out the dear and quiet hills of home.

O fresh as morning, near as pulsing breath,
    Familiar as the touch of clinging hands!

O sad as parting, wild as lonely death,
   Elusive as mirage in desert sands!

Home is a land where gleaming rivers roll
   Which far we glimpse in ecstasy of pain.
Home is the sun-drenched Nowhere of the soul
   That exiled hearts forever seek—in vain!

ELEANOR JORDAN HOUSTON

Eleanor Jordan Houston (Mrs. Aubrey F. Houston) was born in South Carolina and educated at Winthrop College and the College of William and Mary; since 1925, she has taught English in the Los Angeles schools. She is President of the Poetry Society of Southern California, and is a member of the Executive Board of the Chaparral Poets, a widely known Southern California organization.

THE GLASS BLOWER

He blows his dream into the sea-blue glass—
The vision of perfection in a bowl;
And as he blows, the lustrous molten mass,
From smallest particle to rounded whole,
Responds to that frail image which he keeps—
Translucent beauty flows, part cloud, part clear.
A breath too strong, the growing bubble leaps
Beyond the imagined pattern; flaws appear.
Although the impetuous, swirling vessel breaks
Into a thousand useless bits, the sun
Of faith still lights his dream. Again he takes
A mobile globule; confident as one
Who dips into the cosmic pool of thought,
He works until the perfect form is wrought.

IGNACE M. INGIANNI

The son of an immigrant Sicilian family, Ignace M. Ingianni came to America at an early age from a sunny southern land whose warmth and color still burn in his blood. Though he passes his working time in the prosaic task of examining titles for New York City, his spare hours are given to poetry and painting, for he is accomplished with the brush and palette no less than with the pen. His poems have appeared in almost all the better verse magazines; his first book, appropriately entitled *Songs of Earth,* was published in 1938.

THE SEA

Your thunderous dirges strike a chord in me,
For I was cradled by a gusty shore;
I followed ships until my eyes were sore.
And heard the sailors tell of treachery.
They called you devil, when their tongues were free,
Yet at the dawn their skiffs will sail and oar
Were scudding seaward; and the waters bore
The songs of men who hungered for the sea.

Beyond white breakers crashing endlessly,
Beyond the heaven's storm-distracted dome
Where cold fogs gather and the sea-gulls shriek,
There dwells a silence, a serenity;
And they who dare the Titans of the foam
Tremble, but hold the secret when they speak.

LONELINESS

Alone I walk a trackless land
And follow barren streets,
I circle round and start again
For lost unreal retreats.

The world is dead and silence sleeps,
The stars and moon are pale.
In fog I move with phantom feet
Across a misty vale.

The roads keep going on and on
And none there be that end
Until perchance we meet again
Upon some fated bend.

Until again our limbs can spread
Like wings in eager flight
And climb beyond the range of man
And see beyond his sight.

But now I walk with heavy feet
Upon a misty land
And you are far, so far away
And none can understand.

MARY CECILE IONS

Letter to the Dead in Spring was chosen by three nationally known judges for first place in a nation-wide contest conducted by *Wings, A Quarterly of Verse* in 1935; and was subsequently reprinted in Thomas Moult's *The Best Poems of 1935* and many other publications. The author, who graduated from the University of Alabama with Phi Beta Kappa honors and subsequently taught English and French, was living in Coral Gables, Florida, at the time of the award. She has contributed other poems to the magazines.

LETTER TO THE DEAD IN SPRING

Do not be fretful of your old repose
Though April sunlight warm your hearts' dust through
And fragrance of the everlasting rose
Assail the grave and penetrate to you.

The world is greatly altered since you died
And earth took back your strong simplicity.
The iron slaves we fashioned in our pride
Are now our lords—we dreamed of being free,

Forgetting how you joyed to plow and reap
With mighty hands, or drunk with cloud and star
Saw visions while you watched beside your sheep.
We and the world are shrunk; no place is far;

No island undiscovered; even the skies
Are probed by men who mount on clamorous wings,
Yet more to earthward turn their hearts and eyes;
Oblivion keeps the beauty of the things

You found in your own minds. We marvel how
You breasted your world's darkness unafraid,
Drank pain, and kissed life's lips, and died; for now
Grown cold and faint, we fear to be betrayed,

And from time's gifts, like cravens, choose the least.
No longer do we pray for fruitfulness,
Strong with creative joy at marriage feast:
You are the fertile ones, and we are less

Alive than you, whose golden flame of thought
Burns dim in us. O David, who can sing
As once you sang, and who of us has wrought
Like Angelo? Our youth and strength we bring

In our new age to intricate arts of death
Or turbulent commerce; futilely we spend
Your far-descended legacy of breath,
And lose your hope, but cannot make an end

Of your despair. If sometimes old unrest
Broods in your dust in springtime, turn your eyes
And see us whom you raised from earth's dull breast
By strength of your desires, and hear our cries—

Children aghast before the fall of night.
See how the gains you treasured year by year,
As you forever climbed toward peace and light,
Are given again to darkness and to fear

And let your powerful prayers confuse and mock
All evil forces, rising till God stills
The pagan voices whispering, "Ragnaröck",
And bids us lift our eyes unto the hills.

Then dream of earth-forgotten beauty; deep
In all the tranquil wisdom of the dead
Drown your brief longing, murmuring in your sleep
A grace to God for rest, as once for bread.

Leslie Nelson Jennings

For more than twenty years Leslie Nelson Jennings has
been prominently associated with American poetry. His work
has appeared in a host of magazines, including *The New
Yorker, Nation, New Republic, Saturday Review of Liter-
ature, Saturday Evening Post, Commonweal*, etc. He was at
one time a regular contributor of reviews to the *New York*

Sun; and he has held various editorial positions, including associate editorships on *Current Opinion* and *Poetry Chapbook*. A native of Massachusetts, he spent some of his early years in California, where his association with George Sterling and other literary figures marked the beginning of his writing career. He is the author of one book, *Mill Talk and Other Poems,* in which he presents a wealth of insight and observation with the restraint and finish of a practiced hand.

STRANGE MEETING

Loneliness has two faces: one that looks
Aghast on bleak, interminable hours,
And one whose eyes are full of woods and brooks
And a wind-woven plenitude of flowers.
Often I have gone blindly out among
The hills, forgetful of their strength to bear,
Crushing a bitter aloes on my tongue,
Hugging the stony shoulder of despair.

Loneliness has two faces: kind and stern.
In solitary places I have seen
The poor mad woman crouching where the fern
Covers forsaken graves and secret springs,
Her brow untroubled and her heart serene;
And we have spoken there of many things.

WILDERNESS

I have seen wildernesses made,
Trees close their gap 'twixt house and wood;
The grass triumphantly invade
Acres where once the cornstalk stood.

Apples from hillside orchards drop
Ungathered where the nettle thrives;

Bees carry from the clovertop
No spicy honey for the hives.

Yet in such places one may find
An older industry than ours,
A Harvester whose brows are twined
With watercress and meadow flowers.

Neither in envy nor in wrath
Has he retaken this domain,
Jealous of how the scythe's wide swath
Proclaims a season's golden gain.

I have seen wildernesses grow
Where streets were thronged and windows burn,
Where shuttles weave and thistles glow,
Speeding whatever wheel will turn.

Some thriftier husbandry may lurk
Where no one comes to guide the plow,
And I would trust its handiwork
A hundred years from now!

DEEP WOODS

If it were so—a sudden turn in the track
And the cool gloom of the deep woods descending,
No questioning of the way, no looking back
From quietude unbroken and unending—

Then I could understand what it might mean
Walking softly on brown fern long bedded,
Silence by the spring and moss eternally green;
These are not things mysterious or dreaded.

After the dusty road and the heat of the sun,
To slip securely into such secret places,

Knowing that here the red fox need not run
From huntsman or hound forever on his traces.

That would be nothing to fear, though I wandered, lost,
Farther than Summer under the dark boughs bending,
Feeling the brittle solitude of frost,
And the chill gloom of the deep woods descending.

JOSEPHINE JOHNSON

Josephine Johnson, co-President of the Poetry Society of Virginia, is a native and resident of Norfolk. She has published one book, *The Unwilling Gypsy,* a winner of the Kaleidograph Book Publication Prize for 1936; her poems have appeared in *Harper's, American Mercury, Saturday Review of Literature,* and other magazines, as well as in Thomas Moult's *Best Poems, The Home Book of Modern Verse,* etc. In 1936 she was made an honorary member of Phi Beta Kappa by the College of William and Mary.

CHILDREN OF EARTH

(Potter's Field)

O homeless dust, within this green field hidden
Lies home at last, your ancient home and true!
The roof is wide, and though you come unbidden
Long, long ago the bed was made for you.
Here are no questionings and no reproaches;
Only the little creatures of the grass
Shall pause a while to see what guest encroaches,
Then go their way and let the stranger pass.

Cool clay shall heal the lips once harsh with curses,
Fear-stiffened eyes be closed against the night;

No more the piteous, groping mind rehearses
Each grief and terror of its hapless plight.
Only the silence and the warm sweet clover,
The sun, the cloud, the pure effacing snow,
And the long cadence of the wind blown over—
These be the pulse and rhythm you shall know.

Sleep soundly then, with all mankind for brother,
One in the wide democracy of death;
Swelling the dark womb of the first great Mother,
Safe in her side from whom we all draw breath!

CULLEN JONES

Cullen Jones was born in Nevada in 1890; graduated from Stanford University in 1916; was commissioned in the United States cavalry in the same year; and retired in the Twenties as the result of a polo injury. Subsequently he became master of English and head of the Department of English in various private schools, until his recall to active service in 1940. He is at present serving a General Staff assignment, with the rank of lieutenant-colonel.

Despite the exactions of war work, he has continued to produce poetry, which has constantly grown in scope and depth. In 1944 alone he appeared in thirty-five publications, including the *Atlantic, Commonweal, New York Times*, etc.

SONNETS IN WARTIME

While Life Sits Idly

Out of the pillaged dark that makes no moan,
Nor sighing breath to move these autumn leaves,
Nor whispered word to bring again the tone
Of peaceful living to these dripping eaves,

There come illusions marching in parade
On endless roads that bridge no gap nor void,
Demanding that destruction be obeyed;
While life sits idly listing things destroyed.
And who am I? what victim to cajole?
Upbraiding summer's loss and winter's gain;
Reciting as each moment takes its toll
Where horror dances as a thing insane,
"Under this tranquil-sky the earth is still;
It must be I and not the world that's ill."

I Gained a Greater Strength

There in the half-dark of the winter wood,
With wandering flakes designing silver lace,
Where blood-red pools of autumn's death still stood
Warming the evergreen's slow-whitening base,
It seemed as if a neighbor's friendly face
Were pressed against a pane; I knew his smile.
And with that mood the quiet dusk kept pace,
Slowly enveloping, thus to beguile
The sketch in black and white it traced the while;—
Who knows the wisdom of returning youth?—
There was my pictured past for mile on mile:
Each symbol formed its arabesque of truth,
Standing between me and the muraled light:
I gained a greater strength though lost in night.

LEILA JONES

Leila Jones, who lives in Fairfield, Connecticut, won the
Van Rensselaer Prize for lyric poetry at Columbia University
in 1934. She is the author of two books of verse, *Assent to
Autumn* (Stephen Daye) and *Winter is a Shadow* (Dial

Press); and her delicately molded poems have appeared in various magazines and anthologies.

COLOUR OF OCTOBER

Now let the heart that gazed, remember
This day, laden with lovely light;
Summer's last yellow-burning ember;
Gold on the bluebird's wing in flight,
Sleek gold on boughs, gold on the meadow,
And brooks are rimmed with amber shadow.

I said, "By this gold brink of seas
So vast and clear, one might embark
To some undreamed-of Atlantides,
Moving forever through the gold
Where day and evening and the dark
And restive seasons never pass;
None knows regret and none grows old,
Nor years run wasting through Time's glass.
The port (they tell) is never found,
Nor drowsy keels glance on the sand,
Since all of perfectness laps round,
With bounties for the trailing hand."

Now earth rides anchored to a dream,
And I no fairer tale may tell
Of countries set beyond the stream,
Nor Time provide a citadel
More bright for wishful hearts to hold
Than this day hung with autumn gold.

CONNECTICUT TRILOGY

These roads that run from Redding Ridge to Kent,
Up Greenfield Hill and down by Muddy Brook,
Were tangled trails where wandering cattle went,

Or lovers in the twilit April took
Through laurel fields or homeward through the snow.
There by the fire, too diffident to kiss,
They sighed for love, yet when the hearth burned low,
Bundled to bed and thought it not amiss.
So simply is a road begun: a lane
To wander, deep in mint or meadow-rue;
A trail in Autumn lost in leaves and rain;
Faint as the phantom trace on snow and blue
As hillside mist—where in the starlight hush
The dark fox trailed his silver-feathered brush.

More lovely than autumn in Connecticut
Is winter, when the great snows thickly fall.
The granaries are filled; the barns are shut.
Here is a world reversed! Here snow is all!
From a drowned land washed white there bleakly lift
Dark crooked boughs like spars; a wave-swept stone;
A roof-top stranded on the sleeping drift;
Or ragged creeper where a wall went down.
On nights of windless moons the great elms cast
Their shadows on the snow in lengths of lace—
Blue dreamy boughs, mysterious and vast.
But upward in the trees' majestic grace
High on the black and naked heaven, far-swung,
On every bough a blazing star is hung.

These hills were ancient when the Ark went forth
On her strange watery errand in the world!
This stone the oxen brought to build my hearth
Was shagged with moss before the Pequot hurled
His flinty death along the Saugatuck.
Not strange—on this unyielding soil that men
Grew stern or measured Sunday by the clock,
Who dragged their hearthstones down from Devil's Glen
Or harnessed rock to bound an orchard by;

Accepting April with a mind austere;
Grappling with winter lest the cattle die!
Men prudent, sturdy, of a character
Akin to rock or cedars straitly grown,
Unshaped by winds, where roots lie deep in stone.

Thomas S. Jones, Jr.

"The life of Thomas S. Jones, Jr.," declares his friend John
L. Foley in the introduction to Jones' collected poems, "was
that of a dedicated artist who despite the confusion of a
changing age kept a course true to the Ideal." It would be
difficult to find anyone less affected than was Jones by the
pulsings and surgings of the external world, or by the storm
and chaos within the universe of art; as calmly as a medieval
anchorite, he devoted himself to rounding the perfect stanza;
and the result is a body of work consummate in construc-
tion and charming in context even if at times a little remote,
like a scene painted on a canvas. Most of his later poems are
sonnets, of which the great majority deal either with little-
known saints or with eminent historical characters.

Jones was born in Boonville, New York, on November 6,
1882; graduated in 1904 from Cornell, where he and George
Jean Nathan were voted the students "most likely to become
celebrities"; and spent most of his life in New York, as a
reporter, an editor and a poet. He died on October 16, 1932.

SPINOZA

White lilacs blossom by his cottage gate
And song of thrushes floods the lowland lane,
He grinds the crystal with a pointed plane,
Brooding the mystery of man's estate.

On him the star-rimmed heavens do not wait:
  Dawn gleaming red above new-fallen rain,
  The purple twilight with her silver train.
Roll by in splendor heedless of his fate.

But into light resolves the tragic gloom;
  With knowledge and a love beyond desire,
    His soul emerges resolute and free.
The universe flows round his narrow room—
  Lit by the sun and moon's revolving fire,
    Filled with the wild breath of the wandering sea.

LEONARDO DA VINCI

I

The Ride to Milan

Glistening riders, beautiful bright lords,
  They spur through meadows in a foam of flowers
  On toward the city hung with proud white towers,
Vermeil their mantles, damascened their swords;
One rides ahead—his silver stallion fords
  The swiftest torrent—one whom dawn endowers,
  Leonine, lonely, conscious of strange powers:
Life is his lyre of seven flaming chords.

With great glad voices echoing through the trees,
  Carefree they ride, their plumes with dew impearled,
    Above them clouds of light and shadow roll;
While he is silent—he alone who sees,
  Outlined in fire against an unknown world,
    The shifting chiaroscuro of the soul.

II

The Soul of Leonardo

An old god who has taken mortal guise,
  A bright destroying seraph, through despair
  Loosens his bolts of bronze upon the air,
And watches men and beasts that agonize;
At his command, the channeled rivers rise,
  Swayed by a mystery the moon can share,
  And wings of swan-white splendor wait to bear
A fallen angel burning for the skies.

No earthly landscape haunts this Florentine—
  Of dream-like cities he is architect,
    And on his page bloom rose and asphodel;
These flame-lit shapes, by shores of twilight green,
  Flow from the beauty of an intellect
    Fed by the fires of heaven—and of hell.

THE VASE OF MYRRH

In cerements of painted linen wound,
  The Pharaoh in his royal sepulchre,
    As tribute to the dark god's messenger,
Poured rich libations on the burnished ground;
So he whose body by a Dream is bound
  Within life's golden house a prisoner,
    Treasures a vase of sandalwood and myrrh
To offer death's great angel, shadow-crowned.

And when the Spirit long-awaited stands
  Before the entrance to the open tomb
    And finds the cerements of clay unrolled,
Then shall the lover pour within Love's Hands
  Desire and Dream in bitter-sweet perfume
    From life's bright vase of porphyry and gold.

DOUGLAS V. KANE

Douglas V. Kane, who was born forty-two years ago in New York City, has spent the past sixteen years in San Francisco. He was employed for a considerable period in the Portuguese Consulate in that city, although he has no Portuguese blood; more recently, he has been doing war work for the Southern Pacific Railroad. His poems, which are marked by a tenderness and lyrical restraint, have appeared in a number of publications, and have been collected in his volume, *Heart's Wine.*

ON THE FERRY

I gazed with faith upon the sea,
And thought, within my heart,
"The waves, the hills, the winds are *Thee,*
And man Thy filial part."

Then on my ears there broke the slow
And guttural speech of men;
They lived through all the twisted show
Of toil and greed again.

Their words were like the flecks of dust
That soil a wholesome air;
I felt the weeds of hate and lust
Press flowers, virgin-fair.

And though I gazed upon the sea,
I lost my *deeper* sight;
Choked by the mob's mind-harlotry,
My heart was drowned in night. . . .

But still I looked along the waves
And felt the freshening spume,

As one whose sickened spirit craves
A purge from creeping doom.

And finally, by force of will,
My smothered heart was clear;
I watched the breadth of Nature fill
With its eternal cheer.

I thought of women, vestal-eyed,
Who kept the inner fire,
Whose votive love had never died
From tangles of desire.

I thought of men as clean as Truth,
Who stood in knuckled pause,
To strike with blows of mental youth
Defilers of their cause.

All this, and more, came back to me;
The drone of filth was hushed
Within my mind, and the glad sea
Along the gunwale rushed!

Once more I knew man lived as part
With wind and sea and hill,
Of the bright Godhead, and my heart
Again lay in His Will.

CATHLEEN KEEGAN

Cathleen Keegan (Cathleen Keegan Beck) was until recently a resident of Jackson Heights, New York. For a

number of years her poems, some of which show a remark-
able force and depth of feeling, have been appearing in
various magazines.

THREE SONNETS

Temptation

I

What if there is no "Someday" in God's ken,
No sequel to the hours that you and I
Have tried to make unstained and white? Ah, then
What use denied, the love we now deny?
If sacrifice, like sterile seed, we sow
In barren ground, and you and I be made
The fools of fate, what harvest will we know?
Love would be but an instrument unplayed!
If there is no Tomorrow, why not let
Our passion burn its destined way to dust? . . .
(Is this fulfillment, dearest love?) . . . And yet,
Because, despite my doubt, I still must trust,
     Ah, stoop, a moment only, to the bliss
     Of one small sin, the glory of a kiss!

II

If thus my heart should summon you again
To dear reality—though I have kept,
Till now, my vow of silence—would my pain
And all the searing tears that I have wept,
Since last we met, be not enough to pay
For one glad kiss? Or would God's angel send
Another fallen star to mark the way
Our souls would tread unto a bitter end?
What if we gained our right to Paradise
Each striving through this world of dark alone? . . .

One backward step might make of sacrifice
A sacrilege we never could atone . . .
    One kiss might still destroy love's star-set goal
    Though we had paid a thousand times its toll!

Renunciation

How more than blind the hooded fates to weave
So sere a skein; to wing two hearts with fire
Of ecstasy and melody . . . then leave
To human wills the quenching of desire!
I did not hide love from your loving eyes,
Nor do I whisper nobly, "I will go,"
Then teach my lips such trite and songless lies
As, "Happiness will come through doing so."
This way I give you up: Against the blades
Rebellion lifts in myriad array,
I raise a sword whose clean strength surges . . . fades . . .
And wins again . . . till I have cut my way
    Past you, and love, and toward Tomorrow's mark
    Go stumbling, stricken, blinded, through the dark.

Joseph Joel Keith

Joseph Joel Keith, Pennsylvanian by birth and Californian by adoption, has been for a number of years a resident of Los Angeles. His name has gradually been making itself known to readers of the magazines, to which he has contributed prolifically; his two books, *The Proud People* (1943) and *The Long Nights* (1944), have won wide commendation. His work is at its best in his gentler moods, wherein he can write with a touch of unusual tenderness and pity.

THE LITTLE PEOPLE

The little people of the world
Came knocking, knocking at my door.
The little ones, like lonely wind,
Kept whispering of the conqueror.

The little people did not weep;
They were too tired to weep for me.
But, always through the restless night,
I heard them trudging wearily.

The little people had no home.
They fled and fled. I raised the blind.
I lit the hearth; it warmed their hands.
The callers warmed my heart and mind.

LONELY TREK

There is no haven past the sky and sun
if earth ignores the weeping ones who go
throughout great lands where the lonely trek's begun
when greed's the foe.

There is no beauty even in green lands spread
far from sea unto sea if hunger crawls
a promised mile beyond the living dead
where the buzzard calls.

Earth is the heaven where hearts must seek and find
beyond the flaming wilderness of fear,
the cooling stream in meadows of the mind,
and a sweet peace here.

LET US NOT SAY THE SKIN IS DARK

Let us not say the skin is dark.
The hand is dark that flays
the helpless one who has no voice,
who has no right to cry aloud
in evil days.

Let us not say the skin is dark.
The heart is dark that feels
the love for his own child, but gives
no balm for colored, broken ones
he never heals.

Let us not say the skin is dark.
There is no thing as black
as mind that cuts its loss and sin,
as man who cuts ungodly shame
in his brother's back.

MINNIE MARKHAM KERR

Minnie Markham Kerr, of Cleveland Heights, Ohio, has been writing verse for about twenty years. She was one of the organizers of the Ohio Poetry Society, and was its President from 1934 to 1936; in 1940 she was awarded the gold medal for Ohio by the National Poetry Day Committee of the New York Exposition. Her book, *This Unquenched Thirst*, appeared in 1938.

NOCTURNE

There is a stillness in the heart of night,
Made up of sounds so infinitely small,

Strung on a scale so delicately slight,
The ear is not attuned to hear them all.
Yet, listening, I have been content with these:
The wind's low whisper and the quiet mirth
Of leaf and blade; the restless pulse of trees
Riding at anchor in the restraining earth.

These and a thousand other sounds that make
Scarcely a ripple in the tranquil air,
Send countless echoes thronging in their wake;
Outspreading arcs that eloquently bear
The muted tones of some far-distant sea
Whose murmuring shell the night holds up to me.

INEZ BARCLAY KIRBY

Inez Barclay Kirby is a native of Brooklyn, New York; was educated at Berkeley Institute and Smith College; and lives at Bethesda, Maryland. She has had more than four hundred poems published in periodicals; has won numerous literary prizes; and is the author of one book, *River Lights,* whose poems are, as described by a reviewer in the *Washington Post,* "lyrical, inspirational, and born of deep feeling and thought. Their architecture is dignified; they show fine workmanship."

SILENCE

They know not silence who have never heard
The vast, deep-welling soundlessness arise
On mountain peaks that lean against the skies.
Unuttered thoughts seem audible. A word,
Half whispered, rends the stillness as a bird
With dipping wings can shatter, as he flies,

The shining mirror of a pool that lies
In secret forests where no wind has stirred.

They know not silence who have never learned
To seek it on the heights above the hum
Of little busy wings, above the song
That threads the leafy glen. He who has turned
His footsteps toward the clouds and who has come
Alone—will enter silence, deep and strong.

BRIGHT DELUSION

O, Sea of many songs, whoever hears
Believes the music made for him alone.
He leans to the wind and strains attentive ears
To catch the ripple's faintest undertone
With head upflung, he hears the surges roll
In living thunder, while his eyes grow dim
With half-glimpsed revelations which his soul
Exults to dream the ocean shares with him.

Briefly he glows with arrogance and power,
The one accepted lover of the sea—
The tide runs darkly out; his golden hour
Chills to the whisper of eternity.
Tomorrow whose will be the flattered ear
That finds the music intimately dear?

NIGHT UNTO NIGHT

There is a glory setting him apart
Who loves the heavens and through the lonely night
Watches and wonders. Throbbing in his heart,
Celestial rhythms ring for his delight.
He lays a finger on the wrist of space
And feels the secrets of the stars transpire;

Explores the frigid ray that lights his face
And finds, amazed, its source in primal fire.

He trembles at omnipotence revealed
In matter forged and piloted by law.
Re-thinking thoughts millenniums concealed
From human mind, his spirit kneels in awe.
Speak and he does not answer. In his eyes
A morning shines where other suns arise.

THE WELLS OF OUR FATHERS

I plead that the ancient wisdoms
    Avail in the earth again
When stars leaned low in the silence
    And spoke to men.

When the shepherd lone on the mountain,
    Wrapped in the sweet wind's breath,
Pondered the things of living,
    The things of death.

When the body was more than raiment
    And in the sweat of his brow,
Man ate and held good the labor
    With net and plow.

When the strong one was to his brother
    A hiding-place from the wind
And a desert rock's great shadow
    To him that sinned.

We thirst. Let the old pure waters
    Assuage the fever of men;
Let the long-sealed wells of our fathers
    Be digged again.

Herman Eugene Kittredge

Herman Eugene Kittredge has the distinction of being not only a successful practicing physician (he is a specialist in dermatology in Washington, D. C.) but a capable poet. One of his contributions appeared years ago in that celebrated anthology, *The Lyric Year,* and he has since been represented in numerous poetry magazines. His collection of poems, *With Trope and Melody,* reveals a keen imagination along with uncannily Poe-like touches.

THE LAUGHTER OF THE SPHERES

If not a human being lived on earth,
   Four seasons would enact their yearly play,
   The star-strewn solemn dome pale into day,
The spendthrift sun toss down his warming worth.
Around this puny dust-mote's lonely girth,
   From trillion and quadrillion miles away,
   Light's arrows would still hit the target clay
That Chance, five billion years ago, gave birth.

Man thinks earth great and, made for him alone,
   Moves but to tote an infusorium!—
   A mite upon a "grain of sand and tear"!—
So far from nowhere in light-years unknown
   That thought wanes thoughtless, and all words are
     dumb. . . .
   I hear strange laughter, ringing sphere to sphere!

Alexa Lane

The poem quoted below appeared eleven years ago in *Wings, A Quarterly of Verse* and was reprinted by Thomas Moult in *Best Poems of 1934.*

GHOST

I know now how it feels to be a ghost,
Slithering down the chill damp lanes of night,
Blown like the spray along some lonely coast,
Lost in the dark, and vanished in the light;

Pausing to lean against a shutter's lock,
Thinking to enter there and drink a toast . . .
Having no fleshly hand to sound a knock
Or lift a glass to satisfy a ghost;

Turning away—mad for unhaunted sleep . . .
Having no body that a bed could hold,
Having no warm and heavy tears to weep,
Having no age—and being eons old;

Whispering husks of words that rattle—hollow,
Whimpering at the thin blue edge of dawn,
Hugging a flame too pale for moths to follow,
Calling your name . . . knowing that you are gone.

LAWRENCE LEE

Lawrence Lee was born in Montgomery, Alabama, in 1903; attended the University of Virginia; did magazine editorial work in New York; spent some time abroad in Budapest, Vienna and Paris, and returned to America to teach French at the University of Virginia. While at the University he was for a time editor of the *Virginia Quarterly Review*. He is the author of *Monticello and Other Poems* and *Summer Goes On,* and of the earlier limited editions, *A Hawk from Cuckoo Tavern, This Was Her Country,* and *To-Morrow*

Good-Bye. At present he is serving as a lieutenant in the United States Navy on active duty somewhere in European waters.

THE LETTERS

I

Autumn has changed to spring since I last wrote.
There should be stars out where you walk to-night.
To-morrow your blue eyes will fill with light
From open fields, sprung greenly to the note
Cried by new birds that hop about the loam,
And from new heavens shining in the sun.
I wish that my long time away were done,
For I am lonely now and sick for home.

If from some heavy woe the heart might break—
But it will hold with such small griefs as this
And know a hundred newer things to miss.
I would not utter sorrow—for your sake—
But must, remembering morning in your face,
Being from you, alone, in a strange place.

II

This is the season when I think of flight,
Hungry for earth, green country, and deep sky,
Eager to muffle with woods the world's loud cry
And shut my eyes with hills against its sight.
I think how, where you are, deliberate creeks
Make music in the silence as they steal,
How spirit there on quiet ground might feel
The little touch of safety that it seeks.

O, so I think; but there are no escapes.
Flight does not leave the noisy heart behind,
Nor darkness shut the straight eyes of the mind.

The world is with us still in our own shapes,
And all the coverts we shall ever know
Are in the midst of happiness and woe.

III

Swimmer in sunlight, what can the quick trout teach?
Even the swift are taken by surprise,
With wonder captured in their staring eyes.
All that we count as safe is in death's reach.
Calm are the pools of the mysterious streams
And shadowed deeply by the fallen boles,
Yet terror travels with the silver shoals
Like dread with beauty moving in our dreams.

What little hooks of worry time can throw
To take the young and splendid as its catch!
Even the true for time is not a match,
Nor are the little mysteries that we know.
We can but peer in shadowy deeps and watch
The years like startled minnows gleam and go.

IV

I shall forget what seasons have burned blue,
Sending the blown rains whipping down the sky,
And shall remember azure in your eye
And that a deathless summer burns in you.
How shall it be to put this beauty by
When all the body's lovely use is through?
Uncertain, I shall write the joy I knew
And keep you with the summers when we die.

This side of death I had forgot what sweet
The hiving years can store within their comb.
But now the buzzing thought, in turning home,
Finds all the roads of earth with bloom complete

And gathers honeyed memories in its sac
And straightly flies with summer on its back.
To find the south the mind need only turn

V

Where lines of wild ducks point into the gloam,
Arrowed with pressing hunger to be home.
All yesterday I saw their stout wings spurn
The vacant greyness of the alien sky;
And I am sick at heart since yesterday,
And there is half that I should like to say
Within the startled music of their cry.

Keep still unchanged the country where they pass.
They have been far. They sicken for the sight
And comfort of some loved familiar thing
Before, all spent, they splash in reedy grass.
O, to beat safely in some starry night
With distance done and victory in my wing.

MARION LEE

Marion Lee, Boston born and bred, has contributed many
poems to magazines and newspapers throughout the country,
and is the author of one brochure, *Flame and Song,* and one
book collection, *Stones for my Pocket.* Much of her work is
notable for its epigrammatic terseness of utterance.

RUST ON THE LATCH

There is rust on the latch of poetry's house—
Nobody comes any more:
The sun, the wind, the foraging mouse
Do not use the door.

Shadows are playing at hide-and-seek
Where dreams inhabited;
Only complaining timbers speak—
Song and singer have fled.

Spring and the robin, June and the rose,
The cricket troubadour,
The lashing rain, the sifting snows,
Are chronicled no more.

Ghosts are the only tenants; aye,
And echoes that wake and stir—
Lonely, the pine must whisper and sigh
Without a listener.

Rust on the latch . . . for the dream is done.
The dreamer has gone away;
But the fabrics from which the dreams were spun
Are locked in the house to stay.

RANK AND FILE

Though wide earth's ranks of valor,
Small are her halls of fame—
So countless are the legions where
Duty has signed no name.

MARY SINTON LEITCH

Mary Sinton Leitch has been for years a resident of Norfolk, Virginia, where she is co-President of the Poetry Society of Virginia. She is the author of seven books of poetry and drama; is the compiler of the anthology *Lyric Virginia Today;* and has been represented in standard com-

pilations no less than in leading periodicals. Her work is
predominantly of a lyrical nature, sometimes touched with
graceful whimsies.

THE PHANTOM ROSE

To George Sterling

You sought forever for a phantom rose
That fair and fadeless should adorn your breast.
To that white bloom your singing lips were pressed
In dreams where many an iris river flows
Down sun-drenched hills. At last you knew there blows
For mortal no immortal flower; your quest
Was ended that had led from crest to crest
Of star-hung mountains over desolate snows.
O you whose silver flute or golden horn
Could summon all the sirens from the sea,
How could we know how lonely and forlorn
The search for that one phantom flower could be?—
Until you wrenched forbidden gates apart
To find the rose and wear it on your heart.

WINTER OAK

My oak has lost its choirs
To silence and the cold:
Its brief autumnal fires
Are flickering in the mold:
And, though the winds be bitter
That smite the naked bough,
Yet, thus bereft of summer,
No frost can harm it now.

And I, whose blithe, swift season
Of youth is at an end,
Would stand unscathed by treason

Of lover or of friend:
But oh, the heart that suffers,
The heart that cannot be
To the bleak frosts of winter
Indifferent as a tree.

JESSIE LEMONT

Jessie Lemont (Mrs. Jessie Lemont Trausil) was born in Louisville, Kentucky, but has spent most of her life in New York City. She is the author of two books of poems, and of several volumes of translations from Rainer Maria Rilke, which have been acclaimed as among the most capable yet to appear. In her original work she displays a power of vivid and imaginative writing, which strangely enough—like that of one or two of her promising contemporaries—is largely concerned with themes from the animal world.

AFRICAN NIGHT

Muffled and faint the whispering begins,
Stirring, uncoiling through the dusk again,
The accelerated beating of the rain,
The moaning as of unseen violins.
Shadows swim by as undulant as fins,
Pass one by one, a never-ending chain
Of sinister, dark shapes that long have lain
Concealed—and on each eddying figure spins.

Air hushed and hot as breathing of a fierce
Still beast of jungles crouched to spring, a crash—
Shattering silence; unsheathed, sharply near,
A steel-blue cut of light that leaps to pierce
The lurking Menace with a keen, swift flash
And pin it to the earth as with a spear! . . .

WILLIAM ELLERY LEONARD

William Ellery Leonard, who was born in 1876 in Plainfield, New Jersey, and died recently in Madison, Wisconsin, was among the most curious geniuses in the history of American literature. He was the victim of a psychosis which, acquired in childhood, dominated and overshadowed his life, and which he has described eloquently in this autobiographical *The Locomotive God* (1927). Despite this phobia, which prevented his moving about in a normal fashion, he lived a full and productive existence, as a university professor, as the author of more than a dozen books (mostly of poetry), and as a translator. His work exhibits a peculiar intensity and inner force, which sometimes, as in *The Lynching Bee* (1920), flamed into social protest, and sometimes, as in the long sonnet narrative *Two Lives* (1925), blazed in a realm of personal emotions. The last-named work, from which the following quotations are taken, is concerned with the tragic death of the author's first wife.

SONNET

How little do they know of sorrow, they
Who in the early months of death and dust
In vain commiseration feel they must
Guide their friend's thoughts from what has passed away,
So torturingly fearful lest they say
Aught to remind.—Aught to remind of death!—
As if with every pulse, with every breath,
Death were not talking to him night and day!
But then, when time has led him by the hand
Some kindly footsteps from the grave, and he
Begins at last to look about the land,
Then, witless of the subtle irony,
They name old things and torture him again,
Raking to fire the buried coals in brain.

INDIAN SUMMER

(O Earth-and-Autumn of the Setting Sun,
She is not by, to know my task is done!)

In the brown grasses slanting with the wind,
Lone as a lad whose dog's no longer near,
Lone as a mother whose only child has sinned,
Lone on the loved hill . . . and below me here
The thistle-down in tremulous atmosphere
Along red clusters of the sumach streams;
The shriveled stalks of goldenrod are sere,
And crisp and white their flashing old racemes.
(. . . forever . . . forever . . . forever . . .)
This is the lonely season of the year,
This is the season of our lonely dreams.

(O Earth-and-Autumn of the Setting Sun,
She is not by, to know my task is done!)

The corn-shocks westward on the stubble plain
Show like an Indian village of dead days;
The long smoke trails behind the crawling train,
And floats atop the distant woods ablaze
With orange, crimson, purple. The low haze
Dims the scarped bluffs above the inland sea,
Whose wide and slaty waters in cold glaze
Await yon full-moon of the night-to-be.
(. . . far . . . and far . . . and far . . .)
These are the solemn horizons of man's ways,
These the horizons of solemn thought to me.

(O Earth-and-Autumn of the Setting Sun,
She is not by, to know my task is done!)

And this the hill she visited, as friend;
And this the hill she lingered on, as bride—

Down in the yellow valley is the end:
They laid her . . . in no evening autumn tide. . . .
Under fresh flowers of that May morn, beside
The queens and cave-women of ancient earth. . . .

This is the hill . . . and over my city's towers
Across the world from sunset, yonder in air,
Shines, through its scaffoldings, a civic dome
Of pilèd masonry, which shall be ours
To give, completed, to our children there. . .
And yonder far roof of my abandoned home
Shall house new laughter. . . . Yet I tried. . . . I tried. . . .
And, ever wistful of the doom to come,
I built her many a fire for love . . . for mirth. . . .
(When snows were falling on our oaks outside,
Dear, many a winter fire upon the hearth) . . .
(. . . farewell . . . farewell . . . farewell . . .)
We dare not think too long on those who died,
While still so many yet must come to birth.

LOUISE LIEBHARDT

Louise Liebhardt, a native of Portsmouth, Ohio, has
worked for about fifteen years on newspapers and maga-
zines. She is now city editor of the *San Marino* (California)
Tribune. Her poems have appeared in a number of periodi-
cals, and have been collected in one volume, *Love is a
Thistle*.

NOW WITH THE MOON

This is a night when ghosts come stalking—
Trampling my heart with their soundless feet;
Using the moon as a means to enter
Into the stillness of its retreat.

Now with the moon old loves come marching—
Rocking the night with their weightless tread;
Now with the moon comes a ghostly army
Leaving the graves of the misty dead.

I had forgotten how old wounds quiver—
Boneless fingers unarm the mind;
There is no wall that the moon cannot shatter—
Crushing the heart that was crouched behind.

CAROLYN WILSON LINK

Carolyn Wilson Link was born and raised in Newark, New
Jersey, attended Vassar College, and is married to Henry C.
Link, psychologist and author. Her first book of verse, *Fir
Trees and Fireflies*, was issued by Putnam's in 1920; her sec-
ond, *There Is Still Time* (1944), is a publication of the
League to Support Poetry. She has appeared occasionally in
the magazines, but until recently had not the leisure to con-
centrate upon writing. She lives in Scarsdale, New York.

TO BE ETCHED IN SILVER

I

If we speak less of love, let none suppose
Our hearts to be less loving than before;
A quiet wonder is the love that grows
Year by incredible year, not less but more,
Till what a single shopworn phrase could cover
Becomes our atmosphere, our daily fare,
Our roof by night, and when the night is over,
The unconsidered garment that we wear.

Love is the little music, half unheard,
That interweaves our blackest hour with gold,
Transmutes to song our most prosaic word,
Tempers our heat and blunts the edge of cold;
The air we hum together, secret, proud,
Which we need hardly ever sing aloud.

II

Of every house that I have shared with you,
Which have been many, as there may be more,
I most remember laughter echoing through
And sunshine overflowing on the floor.
Of all the troubles we have met together,
And we have breasted no infrequent storm,
I best recall, not the intemperate weather,
But the eventual fire that kept us warm

So safe, so bright those recollected days,
Possessing them, I find it past belief
That the cold ledger of statistic says
They hold the mortal average of grief,
And half at least of every day was night.
Therefore I know what sun gave all that light.

THE LITTLE DEATH

Always alone in sleep,
    And blindfold in the night,
We navigate that deep
    Which severs light from light.

Blindfold, alone, and bound,
    Trusting the usual tide,
We come to solid ground
    Upon the safer side

Thus nightly we rehearse,
    Waking refreshed and stronger,
That dark each must traverse,
    Lonelier, longer.

LILITH LORRAINE

Lilith Lorraine, a native of Texas, has engaged in various activities: as a high school teacher, as an efficiency expert for a large business firm, as a newspaper reporter, columnist and feature writer, and as one of the first women radio announcers. But she is best known for her literary undertakings: for her establishment in 1940 of the Avalon National Poetry Shrine, which now includes 2,800 members throughout the nation; for her editorship for two years of the poetry magazine, *The Raven;* and for the founding early in 1945 of a general magazine, *Different,* with which *The Raven* has been merged, and of which Miss Lorraine is co-editor. Her own poems, many of which have a unique and other-worldly quality, have appeared in magazines throughout the country, and have been assembled in four books. She is at present a resident of Dallas.

IF HE SHOULD COME

If he should come tomorrow, the Meek and Lowly One,
To walk familiar pathways beneath an older sun,
What king would hail his coming, what seer proclaim his
    birth,
If he should come tomorrow, would he find faith on earth?

If he should come tomorrow, what marvels would he see,

White wings that soar the heavens, great ships that sail the
   sea,
A million spires arising to praise his holy name,
But human hearts unchastened, and human greed the same.

As in the days of Herod, the money-changers still
In God's own House contriving against the Father's will;
His messengers in exile, corruption on the throne,
And all the little company disbanded and alone.

Oh, let him come in glory with all the powers of God,
Begirt with shining legions to rule with iron rod,
Till greed be purged forever from out the souls of men;
Lest he who comes tomorrow be crucified again!

THE OTHER PEOPLE

I know not how, but sometimes I remember
The Other People who were here before.
Before the moon became a dying ember
Their spirits slipped through Time's unguarded door.

While man was yet a beast without the leaven
Of mind that frees a soul and makes or mars,
They woke the sleeping spark with fire from heaven,
They bade him stand erect beneath the stars.

They were a gracious people, always smiling:
Strange was their wisdom, deeper than the grave,
Vast as the stars, and as the moon beguiling,
A two-edged sword to shatter or to save.

Calm were their faces, shadowless and shining;
Man would have nothing of their radiant lore;
They went their way and left my soul repining—
The Other People who were here before.

WHEN PLANES OUTSOAR THE SPIRIT

When planes outsoar the spirit, flying blind,
When ships outsail the dreams that gave them birth,
When towers dwarf the upward-reaching mind,
When wealth is mightier than simple worth—

We almost hear the turning of a page,
We almost know what every seraph knows,
That somewhere on a universal stage
A tiresome play is drawing to its close.

BEULAH MAY

Beulah May, of Santa Ana, California, has been known for years to the poetry-reading public for her poems that have appeared in magazines and anthologies, no less than for her books, *Buccaneer's Gold* and *Cuentos*. She has received literary prizes both here and in England. For eight years she conducted a poetry column in a Santa Ana paper; in 1939 she was appointed collector of the work of California poets for the Huntington Library.

TRAIL'S END

Is this the end of all adventuring:
Of golden mornings when I stopped to gaze
Across a mountain shrouded in blue haze;
Of ardent summers and their blossoming;
Of studios at dusk and songs to sing
By laughing artists gathered round the blaze;
Bright seas of amethyst and chrysoprase;
The desert wind; the hot blood's clamoring?

What if the road has darkened to the west:
The friends I love their high endeavors done
Leave brush and palette and slip off to rest,
The colors dim they blazoned in the sun?
Here is the end where all is manifest—
What is Death's meaning but Life just begun?

Vaughn Francis Meisling

Vaughn Francis Meisling, poet-journalist, was formerly employed by the *Los Angeles Examiner,* and recently has served as a Far Eastern correspondent. The lyric that follows appeared several years ago in an American poetry magazine.

I DREAMT SHE CAME

I dreamt she came as fire and as rose,
Fragrance and light, and leaning o'er my bed
Whispered those burning words none other knows,
And took between her hands my peaceless head;

And kissed. There was a movement in the air
As if the blossoms of the year had blown
Their petals and their odors round us there,
As I awoke, as I awoke, alone.

Hellen Gay Miller

Hellen Gay Miller is a native of Attica, New York, a graduate of Mount Holyoke College, and a resident of Longmeadow, Massachusetts. Her work, which is marked by a keen sensitiveness to beauty, has been published in *Good Housekeeping* as well as in various poetry magazines and anthologies, including Thomas Moult's *Best Poems of 1937*.

IF THERE BE MUSIC

If there be music in that future land
Whose far blue edges lie beyond our knowing,
I shall be wholly reconciled to going,—
For that is language I can understand.
If melodies across those fields be stirred
By lifted wings too light for human hearing
Or tilted planets time their swift appearing
To harmony that earth has never heard;

If some great rainbow-arch, outside our ken
Yet glimpsed long since through sunset colors playing,
Sweep in high chords of song above all praying
Into the perfect sevenfold amen;—
I shall not stop to think that I have died,
But only listen and be satisfied.

J. CORSON MILLER

For more than a score of years, J. Corson Miller has been contributing his poems to the magazines, and during that time has appeared in a majority of the better-known publications. He lives in Buffalo, New York, and is a member of the Poetry Society of America, and an Academy Member of the Catholic Poetry Society. His work, which manifests great variety as to moods and themes and often a tenderness of lyrical utterance, shows little if any of the influence of the modern experimental school.

THE MARKET PLACE

We came at dawn to a market place,
Where merchants cursed and swore;
The lust for gold stained every face,
'Twas here grew roots of war.
And we saw too well how love, locked out,
Could never burst the door.

Turn, Poet, quick! and dream your song,
For One is passing by,
Whose hair is spun from the morning-hills,
Where the great star-choirs die—
Whose face is love's remembrance,
When the winds of autumn cry.

The market men were bluff and strong,
They argued hour by hour;
A wrangling, fighting Babel-throng,
They sold things sweet and sour;
Amid the rushing wheels of trade,
They flaunted pride and power.

Return, O Poet of the singing Lance,
And shield unstained as the moon!
Not here has beauty pressed her feet,
On the way to the King's lagoon.
'Tis only greed that wanders here,
Where the withered lilies fall;
And the halls resound to the laugh of death,
With his mask and funeral-pall.

The coins were clinked from hand to hand,
Lord Bedlam ruled the town;
At every stall and trucking stand,
Dame Dollar wore a crown;

The merry sun climbed heaven's stairs,
As trade went up and down.

O, turn you swift, Crusader, back
To the lands where the lovers are;
To the moon-embracing path of pines,
And the streets of the evening-star,
Go far, go straight, to the studded spires,
Where all earth's dreamers rest;
And a vast, unfathomed music streams
From the heart in beauty's breast.

EDITH MIRICK

Edith Mirick, of Washington, D. C., was from 1929 to 1932 editor of the poetry magazine *Star Dust;* is author of two volumes of verse; and has published in *Ladies' Home Journal, New York Sun,* and other periodicals. She has won prizes from the National League of American Penwomen, *Voices,* and elsewhere; has taught poetics; and has specialized in editing collections of verse. She is now engaged in writing drama; her play *Storm* received second prize in the Stanford University Drama Contest in 1943.

MAN PLOWING

Seeker of far millenniums, stop here.
See where against the upper edge of sky
Which skirts the furrowed hilltop, blue and clear,
A man and horse go by.

Say that the man is plowing if you will,
But I say more: Upon the quiet breast
Of earth his hand indites an epic tale.

See how with measured rhythmic pace he goes
Slowly along the brown slope of the crest,
Unfevered, and content with simple toil.
Here may be medicine for earth's dark woes.
As this man lives, so men
Once lived—and may again.

This bit of earth, this acre is his own
Where heaven's edge can meet the hills unbroken
By prick of spire or walls of serried stone,
Where the wind's voice, the phrases of the bird,
Are audible, words definitely spoken,
Syllables heard.

Here on his hilltop may the nostrils know
Locust and clover, oratorio
Of blended perfume loved by summer bees,
Crab-bloom,—and sweeter than all these,
The glamorous scent of newly upturned loam
Upon this acre which the man calls home.

Aye, say it: This man plowing here has fought
Hunger and cold, known little pestilence
Of worm and locust, hail—frost—drought.
See how his rugged shoulders, in defence,
Are muscled grandly for the Titan task,
How gnarled his guiding arm! He has met pain,
Defeat, gone down, arisen once again
Like Antaeus. What more can a man do?

Silence the hum of motor. Slow the speed
Of journeying wheels. Clear from the lanes of sky
All but the birds. So—let the world go by!
The sure unhurried cycle of the seed,

Love and a little laughter, toil and birth,
Then rest, are all the man has asked of earth;

With this the simple wording of his creed:
To live by soil—rain—wind—and sun,
By what his hands have done.

Search then your heart, and all of earth and sky.
Ponder upon the man before you go.
Between these humble lines he writes may lie
Cure for man's raucous fever, and the sum
Of quested joy—yet more: For aught we know,
That which you seek for a millennium.

MINNIE HITE MOODY

Doubtless to many readers Minnie Hite Moody is better known as a fiction writer than as a poet; yet for years she has contributed poems to some of our leading journals. She is the author of five novels, the latest being *Long Meadows* (Macmillan); she has also published a number of short stories and about a thousand book reviews; and for several years she wrote a column for one of her home-town papers, the *Atlanta Journal*. Her poetry, largely in the sonnet form, is distinguished not only for its technical excellence, but for the range of its subject-matter, its insight and its sympathy.

HOW FRAUGHT WITH STRUGGLE

How fraught with struggle is the craft of words!
The garret was not Goldsmith's only Cross.
Exile and cold and poverty and loss
Made Villon's singing as a wounded bird's—
Still beautiful, but anguished. Strength was given
In some strange way, out of some rarer air,
To Jonson, doubly branded with despair . . .
Surely some Angel guards the spent, the driven,

Who whet their pens against eternal stone,
Then dip them deep in thinning blood to write:
How else could they have labored but in vain?—
Lamb, through a fog half London's, half his own?
Frail, wandering Shelley, toiling in the night?
Milton in darkness; Coleridge in pain?

COTTON FIELD

There is a glory past the heart's believing
In the brown bosom of this acreage;
Here have the labor and the desperate grieving
Of fettered men evolved a heritage
Of hope and beauty out of ageless sorrow—
How many tears have wrought this snowy yield?
A yesterday is but a lost tomorrow
Within the borders of a cotton field.

Yet sun and stars seem strangely closer here
Than to more formal premises of earth:
These furrows have spurned weariness and fear
With the persistency of death and birth
Which brood forever over those who know
Nothing of life but cotton, row on row.

OHIO FARMSTEAD

Under this elm, the wandering Wyandots trod;
Under this rooftree, birth and death have battled;
In this wood cradle, babes have laughed and prattled
Whose dust is one now with the meadow sod.
And what are rifle-hooks above a door,
And scratches as of spurs on rounds of chairs?
Time is the enemy who unawares
Will claim this place; he has been here before
And constantly, whoever else has come;
Dependably, whoever else has gone;

Among the wheat, or in the lane he stands,
Testing too calmly, with a patient thumb
The rusty scythe he has been leaning on,
While indoors old men wait to fold their hands.

COUNTRY SABBATH

Surely the hand of God has spread this peace
To grace His day. There is no turmoil here.
Only new lambs with white, unsullied fleece
Wander down paths the daisies have left clear.
Only the flutter of grass, the sigh of willows,
The idle drifting of a butterfly,
Break on a quietude as calm as billows
Of summer clouds suspended in the sky.

Silently, softly, over drowsy hours,
The day moves on, with neither choir nor bell
To mark its meaning. Only the meadow flowers
Closing at sunset, strangely seem to tell
A radiant difference in the last swift light
That brings the benediction of the night!

JOHN RICHARD MORELAND

To hundreds of poets throughout the country John Richard Moreland is known for the correspondence courses in verse writing which he conducts; to thousands of readers his name is familiar because of his poems which have been appearing in leading periodicals and in anthologies for many years. He was the founder and first editor of *The Lyric,* and is on the staff of *Kaleidograph* and *American Family Magazine;* he is the author of ten books of verse, all of them revealing a simple lyricism revolving about the simple, natural subjects so often neglected by poets of late. At present he is offering free lessons in poetry to service men. He lives in Norfolk, Virginia, where he was born.

LIFE'S CLOUDY QUEST

Time is immovable; it is ourselves that pass
As wingèd things that never find their rest.
Life, like a bird that beats against the glass,
Breaks its frail wings upon time's crystal breast.

THE SEA IS FULL OF LOVELINESS AND TEARS

The sea is full of loveliness and tears,
Mists soft as snow, and spray as keen and cold
As steel; the green of forests, sunset's gold,
April's old wonder and December's fears;
.While huddled round its shores are wooden piers,
And little homes where men and women live
Taking the silver tribute it may give
In curious nets and cunning pounds and weirs.

The sea is full of loveliness and grief. . . .
For I have watched the fishermen go out
With jest and song at dawn's first gleam of light,
And I have seen the storm come like a thief,
Darken the sky and claw the boats about,
And I have heard bitter weeping in the night!

DRIFTWOOD FIRES

On these salt acres glittering in the sun
I gather driftwood starred with barnacles:
Through russet grass the winds like plowshares run,
Piling pale sand against the weathered hulls
Of broken ships. Only a sea-bird braves
These now forsaken beaches, slowly making

A lonely journey where the high quick waves,
White-cowled, are breaking, continually breaking.
Across the water, like an old desire,
The fog-horn wails. I pile the faggots high,
Kindle and set the kelp and wood afire
To watch the rainbow flames leap toward the sky,
While age, life's hound, his long-sought quarry spurns,
To dream the while a driftwood fire burns.

TO ONE WHO WORSHIPPED GODS OF GOLD

A miser till his last quick breath,
Then for a tomb his wealth was given;
Bankrupt he hurried on with death
To beg upon the streets of Heaven.

THEODORE MORRISON

Theodore Morrison, a native of Concord, New Hampshire, was for more than five years a member of the staff of the *Atlantic Monthly*, and in 1932 became Director of the Bread Loaf Writer's Conference, conducted each summer by Middlebury College. He is at present a member of the English Department of Harvard. His poems, some of which exhibit markedly classical tendencies, have appeared in a number of magazines, including the *Atlantic Monthly, Saturday Review of Literature*, and *The New Athenaeum;* his several books of verse have been issued over a period of years.

KINDRED

In a drowsy warmth I lie,
Drawing the bed-clothes round,

While the darkness moans in the sky
　And the rain drips cold on the ground.

At the portal and verge of sleep
　Where the senses loosen and swim
From the rule that day-thoughts keep
　And the cogs that move each limb,

I feel the night and the rain
　And the cold earth sodden and dead
Slide under the lifted pane
　And creep on me in my bed.

I feel on the cold earth's face
　Her creatures older than men,
The quail huddled close in her place,
　The rabbit crouched in his den.

In burrows and caves and nests,
　In holes and crannies of stone,
The numberless earth-brood rests,
　The creatures of horn and bone,

Of fur and antlers and claws
　And quick eyes little and bright,
While the globed rain slides from the haws
　And the stiff cones toss in the night.

In my body are bone and horn.
　My hair and the nails of my hands
Confess that I too was born
　Of the wide earth's fruitful lands.

If I look with awe on the sky,
　If a word strikes pity or fear,
'Tis by that strange glass, the eye,
　Or those waxen caves, the ear

O creatures crouched on the earth
   In this night of phlegm and cold,
We have sprung from the selfsame birth
   In a world that is passing old.

But my life is against your life,
   And the smoke is laid to your dens,
For mankind grows ever more rife,
   And no hands are more cruel than men's.

We have sealed your death with our cities;
   At the mercy of death we live;
And the soul that perceives and pities
   Finds little comfort to give.

But now for an instant's time
   On the portal and verge of sleep,
I behold the ladder we climb
   And I see the watch we keep.

And I would that we both might pray
   To some power vaster than earth
To sweeten the lifelong way
   We tread from our ancient birth.

LEGEND

Makers of fables and of verses tell
And many times have told
Of an imagined country, free from pain,
From weariness, and death, and cold.
It rises in bright meadows from the swell
Of the wind-darkened sea.
No snow falls there, nor hail,
Nor God's contemptuous phlegm, the autumn rain.
The age-old tree

Is riven by no shrill, disheartening storm,
But always in Hesperian light,
Such as on shores beyond the wind and foam
Brightens across dark waves before the night,
That fabled country stands.
It is the mother of all perfect lands
Shaped by the mind or sought in ventures far,
Near as the white glance of a star
Upon the shallows of a meadow stream,
Yet sundered by the frozen gulfs of sky.
And whoso has regarded it in dream,
Or seen its fields with spiritual eye
Shining beyond the windy bay
At the still ebb of day,
Must feel his spirit warm with inward tears,
Must bear through all his years
A longing inexpressible, unsought,
But dear as life, with very life inwrought.
Light is the essence of that fabled land,
Light that is ever present through the world,
Changing as winds and waters change,
Blowing through sea-green grasses over bright sand
And in green caves of breakers curled;
Light the impalpable and strange,
Light the impalpable and strange,
The swift of foot that through the bright leagues races
And visits clouds and in the wild rose sings.
Often from ranging in the world's broad spaces
The swift feet of the light descend
Upon a shore by dark waves breasted.
Then barns and spires and the rich shapes of trees
Are changed, and held immortal, and arrested.
And then across the intervening seas
The meadows of the fabled land appear.
He that beholds them thinks of lover and friend,
Of all that he holds dear.

They throb within his pulse, till they and he
And all the world are lost, and what is real
Is only longing without depth or end,
A strong, sad, burning wish that life might be
Secure, and worthy of men's breath,
A light and recompense for death,
Clear as the fields imperishably clear
And shining in the barriers of the sea.

ROBERT MORSE

Robert Morse was born in Toledo, Ohio, in 1906; graduated from Princeton in 1928 with highest honors in Art and Archeology; won the College Arts Association Prize the same year; and subsequently studied art in France. Since his return to New York, he has been painting portraits and writing articles, book reviews and poems, and has appeared in *The Nation, Poetry,* and other magazines. His most notable achievement is the volume, *The Two Persephones,* composed of a pair of remarkable long blank-verse poems, from the first of which the following passages are taken.

THE QUEEN OF ELEUSIS

The king sat silent in the hall, his queen
beside him, while their daughters huddled close
and listening with circular bright eyes.
The lullaby came welling from within
and filled the twilight volume of the room.
No water ever flowed more cool, no moth
with ferny front had ever flown more soft,
or tide more gently lifted to the moon
pale thirsty seeds, than cool, and soft, and mild,
that secret song possessed their listening ears.

What did they hear, the five who listened there?
For each a different song, a message tuned
to probe and comfort in a private world.
What images arose that seemed to draw
all scattered meanings to a central whole?
The king, he heard a hunting song, and dreamed
or rather seemed to be remembering
a time he stood within a dewy wood
and drew his bow to pierce a moveless stag—
but left the feathered murder unreleased.
And for the girls, who knows what flight and stir
may occupy the secret minds of girls?
what gleam on princes' plumes? what changing glimpse
of yearnings dark and inexpressible?
The queen—whose heart was filled with bitterness,
envious that another's hand was skilled
more than her own to heal her ailing child—
seemed, with that song, to hear her mother's voice
and lie again within her mother's arms.
Then all the rancour raised against the nurse
dissolved and died. The tears washed down her cheek,
and still the nurse sang on, sang on, and scent
of roses intertwined and clasped her song.

PERSEPHONE THE QUEEN

The past keeps watch above the present's sleep,
and sits all night in judgement on itself.
So Pluto, tall above the noisy feast,
reflects upon those vows within his keep
exchanged by lovers when they, furnace-hearted,
sighed for love's union; sweet words breathed by mouths
desired by forecast, but in retrospect
despised; contracts foresworn, when use of time
divided body from the vagrant dream,
and flesh of gods became a daily loaf.

What thigh ungirt by fancy turns the sense
withinward, there to find the counterpart
of dream, which is the only bliss of love?
O curse of love, he mused, that love transforms
the one most loved into some other thing,
and lays a changeling in our eager arms.
Was it to place this talking, kissing queen
beside me on my seat that passionate
I fed the roots of the Sicilian plant
with my own blood? The body's gate unsealed,
must then a hundred golden doors clap shut
that opened into dawn and mystery?
O woman, closed and blunt of sense—save this
which keeps perpetual ambush in my sheets—
now in our one-ness there were never two
so sharp divided in such solitude!

DAVID MORTON

Few if any poets of our time have employed the Shake-spearean sonnet with greater grace and a closer approach to perfection than has David Morton, whose blending of melody and meaning has illustrated anew what magic may remain untapped in the old, often-used forms. Mr. Morton was born in Elkton, Kentucky; has served variously as a reporter, an editorial writer and a teacher; and from 1924 until early in 1945 has been Professor of English at Amherst College, though recently he resigned his position in order to devote his full time to writing and lecturing. He is the author of seven books of verse and two critical volumes, and is the compiler of several anthologies.

MOONS

Some moons the world can nevermore forget,
   Whose nights are one with many a shining name:
The moons of Avalon are silver yet,
   Where towers still wear their moonlit, haunting fame.
And shadows laced on pillared porticoes,
   Where moons were over Athens in the spring,
Will be remembered when the last moon goes,
   A dark, abandoned and forgotten thing.

On nights like this, beyond the solemn hill,
   Tall towns lift up their turrets to the moon,
In this old moving radiance, haunted still,
   With what had been their golden bale or boon,—
With storied names and dim, blue streets to stray,
As when their moon went by the selfsame way.

A KING IN EGYPT

Lift up the shuttered eyelids that were drawn
   On splendid pageantries once pictured there:—
We are too tardy, they are centuries gone;
   There is no road to countries that they fare.
Now heed the pulse if it be swift to change,
   And listen at the lips if still they keep
Some word that once was passionate and strange
   For one who heard . . . and smiled . . . and fell asleep.

He is not desecrate; his life were all
   Inviolate still within his own brief day:
Some joy of swords . . . or April at his wall,
   Music . . . and heartbreak . . . and a name to say
Of one who somehow touched his youth with dream,
And passed, another leaf upon the stream.

MOTHS

Where is it that these frail adventurers go
   That veer so lightly, with so brave a will,
So delicate and strange, that tremble so,
   For all the dusk is windless now, and still . . . ?
Where is there left, in crashing worlds whose wake
   Is strewn with shards of kingdoms shocked and tossed,
A place for things so small as well might break
   Their wings against a twilight, and be lost . . . ?

What kings of earth, no longer now renowned,
   Have gazed at dusk, beyond such shapes as these,
To shadowy empires whence their arms were bound,
   Blind to white moths gone straying through the trees,
Nor thought how all the kingdoms they might cull
Were brief as these—and not so beautiful!

HELENE MULLINS

In 1935 nation-wide attention was attracted to a young poet through an automobile accident that came within an inch of being fatal. Upon her recovery from three weeks of unconsciousness, her sister presented her with a huge stack of letters from unknown readers throughout the country; for Helene Mullins was already known to a wide circle, as much for her poems which had appeared two or three times a week in F. P. A.'s column as for her two books of verse and her novel. She has subsequently published another volume, *Streams from the Source,* written during the three years of her convalescence, and notable, as is all her work, for its individuality and intensity of feeling.

Of the genesis of her poetic efforts, Miss Mullins writes, "It was not until after I left boarding school, at the age of fifteen, that I discovered poetry. Hearing a young man at a party recite *Thanatopsis*, I dashed to the library next day to look for it. From *Thanatopsis* I progressed to *The Raven*, and the complete poetical works of Poe. It was Poe who caused my ambition to switch from that of becoming a story writer to that of becoming a poet."

THIS, TOO

This passion, too, will end at last
Though Time has promised nothing yet.
Unlucky loves sink in the past,
Disconsolate minds learn to forget.

The book of history is filled
With tragic tales of clown and sage,
And I, before my blood is still,
Shall add to it another page.

Let me not therefore dream that I
Feel something strange and something new,
That will not ever fade or die,
That through eternity will be true.

This passion, too, at last will end,
Like any other, and begin
With the teeming universe to blend,
And I shall yield to discipline.

THE MOUNTAIN COMES TO MAHOMET

Be quiet now, my beating heart,
Nor strain so passionately.
Desire will tear me not apart;
The mountain comes to me.

"Your dream is mad, incredible!
You see a moving wraith.
Such wonders are impossible!"
Say men of little faith.

But when desire is strong within
Man's self, and taut and brave,
It must by some procedure win
On time's eternal wave.

Be now at peace, be now at peace,
O heart and straightway see
My ineffectual labor cease;
The mountain comes to me.

GIVE HEED TO THE OLD

Give heed to the old, for they have traveled far,
And the dust of many roads is on their feet.
Absorb their tale of corpse or avatar,
Absorb their tale of conquest or retreat.

Experience has given them many drills.
They know the jagged stones in the vales of grief,
They know the gleam of stars above the hills,
They know how brief is life, how strange and brief.

Give heed to the old within time's final booth.
Long have they gazed upon and fingered deeply
The looms of life that weave illusion, truth,
They know what may be purchased dearly, cheaply.

Gather their smiles and tears before they go
To cast themselves upon a distant shore.
Learn from them how life's waters ebb and flow,
How its runnels sing and how its torrents roar.

Jessie Wilmore Murton

Jessie Wilmore Murton, of Battle Creek, Michigan, has been prominent in the poetic activities of her own state, and is the author of many published poems. She has won prizes from *Kaleidograph, Versecraft, Wings,* and other poetry magazines. Much of her work is in the ballad form, of which an example follows.

BALLAD OF CORONADO'S QUEST

The dawn was on the mountains,
    And wine was in the air,
With mellow peal of trumpet,
    And silver bugle flare,
With horses draped in scarlet,
    And priests in crimson stoled,
And in the luminous distance
The seven fabled cities whose streets were paved with gold!

A monk had brought the legend:
    Far to the beckoning west
Romance! Adventure! Riches!
    But waited on the quest!
But waited Coronado,
    The gallant and the bold,
    The cities of Cibola!
The seven fabled cities whose streets were paved with gold!

The Barb of Andalusia
    Had sired their prancing steeds,
The goldsmith and the armorer
    Wrought well to meet their needs!
To artisan and weaver
    In terms of dream were sold
    The cities of Cibola!
The seven fabled cities whose streets were paved with gold!

And "Ride!" The brave Don shouted,
  His jeweled blade thrust high!
"Ride!" Monk and abbé chanted,
  Eyes lifted to the sky.
(While "Ride!" The Aztec captives
  Spat through tight lips.) "Behold!
The cities of Cibola!
The seven fabled cities whose streets are paved with gold!"

But seas are salt and fickle,
  And long trails bruise and tear,
And pageantry grows tawdry
  On naught but hunger's fare!
Nor armour, even golden,
  Repels the shafts of cold,
O cities of Cibola!
O seven fabled cities whose streets are paved with gold!

The winding rivers mocked them,
  The mountains laughed in scorn,
The prairies, with their vastness,
  The desert, with her thorn,
Left never hoof to enter,
  No eye that might behold
The cities of Cibola—
The seven fabled cities whose streets were paved with gold!

The dashing caballeros,
  The princely Aztec slaves,
The swarthy dons, and prelates,
  Sleep well . . . in unmarked graves! . . .
And in the luminous distance
  Lie, even as of old,
The cities of Cibola . . .
The seven fabled cities whose streets are paved with gold!

John Russell McCarthy

John Russell McCarthy, one of the best-known poets living today in the West, has had a life of varied activity. He was born in Huntingdon, Pennsylvania, November 16, 1889; was educated at Juniata College and Pennsylvania State; was a newspaper reporter and editor in his home town; and in 1920 came to California, where he has lived ever since. He is the author of seven books, the first of which, published in 1918, won him the friendship of John Burroughs; is editor of the series of nine standard historical volumes called *California;* and at present edits the *Camellia House Journal* at La Canada, California. In 1928 he was awarded the John Burroughs Memorial Medal for nature writing. He conducts a regular department in the *Writer's Monthly*, and has contributed poems to most of the better magazines.

I HAVE CURSED WINTER

I have cursed winter when the moon was white
Between white clouds above the white, white snow;
I have cursed winter for his howling death
And for his silent death
And for his fear.

I have cursed sorrow when no tears would come
To ease the smarting of the dry, dry eyes;
I have cursed sorrow for her vanity
And for her emptiness
And for her strength.

Yet on the winds of winter I have come
To April, flower-eyed;
And on the sands of sorrow I have crept
To the clear spring of joy.

NOW I WHO SAW

Now I who saw the splendid sun
  Come riding forth from clouds of gray,
  Making a garden of the day,
I pitied the sightless trees, each one.

I pitied my old friend, the oak,
  Who lacked my eyes and could not see—
(How could he know when rain-dawn broke,
  Poor hapless unperceiving tree?)

And then I saw the old oak tree
  Turn up his leaves like hands on high,
  And greet the sun and praise the sky.
He smiled. I think he pitied me!

Robert Nathan

Prominent both as a fiction writer and as a poet, Robert Nathan is perhaps best known for a long list of novels, many of them notable for their delicacy and finesse of treatment and for the imagination and sympathy they display. Yet it is questionable whether he will not be longest remembered for his poems, the best of which have few rivals in the current scene for their grace and finish of utterance and for the suggestive depths beneath the mellifluous outer flow.

Mr. Nathan was born in New York City in 1894, and is at present with Metro-Goldwyn-Mayer Pictures, of Culver City, California.

THE HEART IN WONDER

The heart in wonder, like a lonely wren,
Will sing a while, and then be still as long.

He waits an answer ere he sings again,
Who sings for love, and not alone for song.
The bird's shy pipe will falter in the end,
The heart's voice sicken if it be not heard,
They seek the absent, the belovèd friend,
Song is for lovers, whether heart or bird.
So, if you hear me, tell me that you hear,
Lest I grow weary and forget to sing;
As in this sweet green season of the year
The bird that hears no answer lifts his wing
And far away, dejected and remote,
Tries other woodlands with his lonely note.

BEAUTY IS EVER TO THE LONELY MIND

Beauty is ever to the lonely mind
A shadow fleeing; she is never plain.
She is a visitor who leaves behind
The gift of grief, the souvenir of pain.
Yet, if a trace of loveliness remain,
It is to memory alone addressed;
That spirit looks for beauty but in vain
Which is not by an inner beauty blessed.
And, as the ebbing ocean on the beach
Leaves but a trace of evanescent foam,
So beauty passes ever out of reach,
Save to the heart where happiness is home.
There beauty walks, wherever it may be,
And paints the sunset on the quiet sea.

TREAD SOFTLY, SORROW

Tread softly, sorrow, for the summer passes,
Her leaves are falling in continual rain;
Let me be silent as the withered grasses,
Let me be quiet as the gathered grain.

This season that inevitably closes,
The swift returning year again will bring;
The summer passes with a rain of roses,
And winter follows, fading into spring.
So let me, like a tree, with natural reason
Put all my buds to bed at winter's start.
Then in the April of another season,
Beauty will break and blossom in my heart,
And birds renew their youth along the bough,
When all is green—my heart remembers how.

THERE ARE FOUR DOORS WHICH OPEN ON THE SKIES

There are four doors which open on the skies.
The first is truth, by which the living word
Goes forth to seek the spirit and be heard;
Lost in the universe, the spirit lies.
Then justice with her veiled and quiet eyes
Stands at the second portal; at the third,
Faith and her sparrow, the immortal bird;
And the last gate is love's, to paradise.
These are the doors by which the mighty pass.
Yet in the wall there is one wicket more,
With rusty hinges and a splintered floor,
A shattered sill half hidden in the grass.
Small is the gateway as the Scriptures tell;
Its name is pity, and God loves it well.

EBB TIDE

So then to bed and bid the world goodnight.
Slow falls the moon across the western slopes;
See how the city in her lonely light
Puts out like lanterns one by one our hopes.

MOUNTAIN INTERVAL

What if these mountains lift their pride
To skies as warm as these, or cold?
The heart must be at least as wide
As this, to have such peace to hold.

The heart must be at least as high,
The spirit have as broad a lease,
To lift such quiet to the sky,
To take the hills with so much peace.

EPITAPH

Say he was sad, for there was none to love him,
And sing his song.
Now he is still, and the brown thrush above him
Sings all day long.

Say he was lost, for there was none to find him,
And hold him tight.
Now the brown hands of mother earth will mind him
All through the night.

JENNIE M. PALEN

Jennie M. Palen is a contributor to *Good Housekeeping*, *Toronto Star Weekly*, *New York Sun*, *New York Herald-Tribune*, and other publications. She lives in New York, where she makes her living as a certified public accountant.

WATER FRONT

Along the water front, in years before,
The creaking ships of commerce lay adrowse,

Craft with the smell of India in their bows,
Ships from Ceylon and sultry Singapore.
And weary clerks, forever tied to shore,
Would come to watch and make their wishful vows
That some day they'd forsake their desks to browse
In tropic isles. Today they clerk no more;
But, armed with guns, in military file,
They take their solemn places at the rail;
At last to visit some far magic isle;
Across the beckoning seas at last to sail.
They taste at last the ocean's salty breath;
At last they voyage—to a joust with death.

DONALD PARSON

Donald Parson was born in Washington, D. C., was educated at Harvard, and at present divides his time between Pinehurst, North Carolina, and Brooklin, Maine. He is the author of two volumes of poetry, the first of which, *Glass Flowers*, went through four American printings and an English edition upon its appearance several years ago; while the second was published in 1944 with a laudatory introduction by Alfred Noyes, who points out that Mr. Parson, unlike so many contemporary versifiers, "did not cut his roots from the past," and did not "attempt to keep in step with the contemporary procession." Unswervingly faithful to tradition, this poet has done his best work in the sonnet form.

THE DEATH OF SHELLEY

In storm he lived and with the storm he died;
Such is the poet's proper course and end.
He makes the world his confidant, his friend
The wave, an Adriatic is his bride.

And if the tempest rises in its pride
To slay the singer of the shining ode,
We must not weep, but bear the sweet-sad load
Like those who gather meerschaum from the tide.
So build a bonfire on some lonely coast,
A few friends watching, but the world apart.
His soul was like a flame, and now in death
The body shall go winging to its ghost,
A cloud, a skylark, and the west wind's breath.
Then let Trelawny snatch the burning heart.

TO AN EGYPTIAN MUMMY

Here is the house from which the tenant fled
Dim years ago into the night alone,
Leaving this monument—a drowsy stone—
To sleep the long siesta of the dead.
No cunning spice of Egypt could embalm
The flaming soul, no myrrh nor linen stay
The spirit's flight; only the patient clay
Endures the hell of an eternal calm.
Yet this grim boulder lived—was once aware
Of dawn, of high noon's laughter, moonlit lust—
Swam in the yellow Nile—was debonair
And vivid. Now it lies, a shriveled hag,
While rude attendants come, and damn the dust,
And wipe a Pharaoh's features with a rag.

SURELY THE AUTHOR

Surely the Author of our little play,
Since He is wise and hath a nimble wit,
Cannot have given us the whole of it
In this dull drama of our life today;
Where lord or lady struts the leading part,
And some unfortunate must act the fool,
And every string-pulled puppet is the tool

Of circumstance, with sawdust for a heart.
I think that when the velvet curtain falls,
When Virtue has been made to abdicate
And lay her crown upon the head of Sin,
Some shining herald (glancing at the stalls
Where sits intelligence) will simply state,
"The Prologue ends. Now let the Play begin."

EDITH LOVEJOY PIERCE

Edith Lovejoy Pierce was born in Oxford, England, moved
to this country upon her marriage in 1929, and subsequently
became a naturalized citizen. She has published about three
hundred and seventy-five poems, in addition to reprints in
newspapers and magazines; is the translator of Philippe
Vernier's devotional book, *With the Master,* now in its
fourth printing; and is the author of one book of verse, *In
This Our Day,* issued by Harper's in 1944. She lives in
Evanston, Illinois.

DIRGE

O sad, sad world, O world that knows not Love,
But fashions shell and armor, spear and nail,
With unrelenting hearts which these entail,
O world of hate, O world that knows not Love.
Light shines; the darkness comprehends it not:
Too swiftly was thy provenance forgot,
O tragic world, O world that knows not Love.
Proud, hard, the city set upon a hill
Denies the humble Rider, weeping still:
O foolish world, O world that knows not Love.
Drives him to death beyond the outer gate,
Unmindful of his high and hidden state,—
O fearful world, O world that knows not Love.

And so the armored years march thousands strong,
While the sick heart still cries, "How long? How long?"
O sad, sad world, O world that knows not Love.

INCARNATION

Blow cold against the flame,
Throw sand upon the spark;
You cannot keep the Light
From shining in the dark.

Hunt out the heedless head,
And swing the acid knife;
You cannot abrogate
The ever-willful Life.

Immure the hallowed Word,
Bring faggot, rack and rope;
You cannot blur the Faith,
You cannot blunt the Hope.
No matter how untamed
Your ill intent may run,
You cannot stop the Pulse
That beats behind the sun.

ALAS, ALAS, THE WINTER

The furtive wind of winter,
The grim nocturnal gloom,
Can never crush nor enter
The closed and happy room.

But joy can hardly prosper
Against war's bitter price—
A candlepoint of jasper
In unrelenting ice.

HARRY NOYES PRATT

One of the West's better-known poets of the past generation, Harry Noyes Pratt was born in River Falls, Wisconsin, in 1879. He was widely published in periodicals and anthologies, although no collection of his poems has appeared since *Hill Trails and Open Sky* (1919). At various times he was editor of the *Western Journal of Education* and of the *Overland Monthly;* from 1936 until his death on May 19, 1944, he was Curator of the Crocker Art Gallery in Sacramento.

THE SEVENTH CITY OF CIBOLA

Where these low walls run fast to desert sand
And roofs long vanished leave but brazen sky;
Where winds unhindered sweep a barren land,
A city's walls rose golden, wide-stepped, high.
Where now the rattler waits in his scant shade
Drowsing across the torrid noonday heat,
A living people sought long crumbled gates
Called by the drum's resurgent, sullen beat.
Here sat the weavers; here the potters made
Olla and urn, deft spun the patterned bowl;
And in the pueblo's purple, square-cut shade
The gamesters watched the carven pebbles roll.
And now the walls are worn to sand, and lie
Low-ridged beneath the vulture's lonely flight.
Silence— Only the wild, thin, far-flung cry
Of a coyote quavering on the desert night.

THE WOOD OF TARA

I heard a tiny hammering as of wee bells a-clamoring,
         From out the wood of Tara.
   And it was just at summer dusk;

The moon was but a withered husk
>> Above the wood of Tara.

I crept soft-footed down the lane, where puddles lingered
>> from the rain,
>> And there by wood of Tara
I saw an elfin forge a-glow,
And sparks from elfin bellows blow
>> A-down the wood of Tara.

An elfin smith an anvil beat, he forged wee shoes for his
>> horse's feet
>> Close by the wood of Tara.
He forged the shoes and put them on,
He leaped to the saddle, away and gone!
>> Into the wood of Tara.

The tired stars were glimmering where dim the road was
>> shimmering
>> By silent wood of Tara.
The night had grown so still, so still;
The moon had dropped into the hill
>> Beneath the wood of Tara.

DOROTHY QUICK

Dorothy Quick, of New York and East Hampton, Long Island, has published several books of poems, has contributed verse to many periodicals, and has written stories for various popular magazines. Her work has appeared prolifically for a number of years.

A SPECIAL PLACE

God has a special place for still-born things,
The things that never were and should have been:
The little songs no singer ever sings,
The beauty of a picture hung unseen,
A noble heart that loved with no return,
And deeds well meant which somehow turned out ill,
A lovely flame that vainly tried to burn
But could not last, though all the winds were still,
The early flower that no one ever sees
Making its way through ground iced hard with sleet,
A Caesar to whom no man bends his knees,
The Christ-like smile that meets each fresh defeat:

God treats them very tenderly for He
Knows what the pain of stifled things can be.

BARRIER

I wept, still hoping tears might be the key
Forged to unlock death's fortress of a door,
Cried out vain pledges to eternity
To be with you for just one instant more,
But there occurred no opening of the door.

Then weeping blurred my eyes, I could not see
Beyond that vast, unconquerable door.
Aghast at what my world had grown to be,
Bloodied and bruised, heartsick, and sore and lost,
I gave up hammering upon the door.

Then at long last your message came, more clear
Than all my pain. "Gaze now upon the door."
I looked—and you were standing very near,
As close as you had ever been before.
There was no door.

Hugh Wilgus Ramsaur

For many years Hugh Wilgus Ramsaur has been turning out capable poetry with little fanfare. His obscurity is due in part to the fact that he has never submitted his poems except to a few verse magazines, and in part it arises from the circumstances of his life. In the buffetings of an unpoetic world against his poetic temperament, he has been employed at various times in a library, a retail book store and a church choir; he has been a substitute mail carrier, a gymnastic instructor, a salesman of athletic equipment, a W. P. A. worker in a city park, and a free-lance singer and banjoist. At present he is working in a New Jersey shipyard.

Mr. Ramsaur's work, small in quantity, is marked by a meticulous devotion to detail; his lyrics and sonnets have a classic finish, and he is one of the few recent writers to achieve success in that difficult form, the quatrain.

WORLD-RUIN

(Suggested by world events of 1940-41)

Ah, what if Time forgot to light the stars,
Weary of viewing our long, senseless plight
Of greed and blundering death, and dawnless night
Sealed with a frozen doom our gaping scars!
Fantastic ice-crags loomed. Colossal spars
Stood fixed in writhing grandeur! Still and white,
A tortured phantom-sea where sound nor sight
Disturbed the avenging dark's unfathomed bars.

And some lone Being lost from outer-space
Should aeons hence feel wonder to behold,
Written with chasmal runes, that a proud race
Could so have fallen; and deep in the mold
Of Conquest's ruined dreams and shattered gold
Find, wrought in stone, an anguished, thorn-crowned face!

GARGANTUA
(To a Steam Shovel)

Like some lost monster of the Saurian Age
Forever made mechanical, you seem;
Steel-scaled, steel-boweled, belching clouds of steam,
Swooping to gore the earth with seething rage,
A fuming pterodactyl in a cage . . .
And yet I'm told you breathe a mighty dream
To scale the air with mortar, brick and beam,
And leave mankind a nobler heritage!

Your clanking, muddy jaws—the wounded soil,
Tell me that soon will rise another tower
Where, hidden from the sun, more gold will pass
And, buried from the world, more men will toil. . . .
Turning away, I see a broken flower—
And stone on stone and glass on leaden glass.

ENIGMA

Time is a withered monk whose pale hands write
By flaring candles of the stars and sun
What mystery? An Age swirls down the night . . .
The candles fade into oblivion.

EPITAPH, FOUND SOMEWHERE IN SPACE

In desolation, here a lost world lies.
All wisdom was its aim: with noble plan,
It sounded ocean deeps; measured the skies;
And fathomed every mystery but man.

THE ABSOLUTE

Life surges from It in an endless sea;
Yet still inscrutable the Secret stands:
No vaster, holding all Eternity,
Than one pale petal fading in our hands.

HOWARD RAMSDEN

Most of Howard Ramsden's poems have appeared in newspapers and in the "little magazines," to which he has made frequent recent contributions of work notable for the delicacy of its lyrical touch and for its buoyant and often elfin imagination. He lives in Leaksville, North Carolina.

ON A GREEN HILLOCK

As on a green hillock
I pluck this wry leaf,
I hear a wee body
To call me a thief.

I see you, Mad Fairy,
As plain as I'd choose.
You sit at yon mullein
To cobble green shoes.

Child of that other land
Under the hill,
Where does Time hurry
The daffodil?

Into the rainbow?
Or down in the tomb?
Through azures of space
  Or that darkest room?

Tell us, the dreamers,
The lonely, the old—
Where does Time bury
His theft of our gold?

LOUISE CRENSHAW RAY

Louise Crenshaw Ray, a lifelong resident of Alabama, has contributed stories, essays and verse to more than a hundred magazines in the United States and England; has written three collections of poems, of which the latest won the Kaleidograph Book Publication Prize for 1944; has appeared in many anthologies; and has been prominent in her own state for her activities in connection with the Poetry Society of Alabama, of which she is a founder and past president.

BUT STILL INTREPID ICARUS

Ah, what are these you draw ashore
    Encrusted with the bitter brine?
A broken wheel; an airman's oar!
    How can a fishing net confine
A wing whose passion was to soar?

What monstrous fate, what demon gale
    Condemned it to the hungry spray?
    Your net has never held a prey
That told so tragical a tale . . .

    But still intrepid Icarus
    Must seek the sun and perish thus.

Lizette Woodworth Reese

Few American poets of this century have been more widely published or more generously recognized than Lizette Woodworth Reese, who first drew widespread attention through her *Tears,* one of the most memorable sonnets in our literature. Despite a considerable poetic productivity and a fair-sized list of books, Miss Reese passed forty-five years as a teacher in the Baltimore public schools, from which she retired in 1923. She was born in Baltimore in 1856, and died several years ago. Her work, which has a fragile lyric quality, deals unpretentiously but often endearingly with commonplace and perennial things: with rain and roses, with dawn and daffodils, with hedges and home, as in the sonnet that follows.

SMALL THINGS

Life, being careful, such a husbandry shows,
As fits into its grasp, no more, no less,
Than it can keep of ancient loveliness;
A province it discards, retains a rose.
What out of times and weathers will it save?
Some small importance of a hedge, a town,
Not worth a corner's gossip, a renown,
But exquisite with the touch of the grave.
What would we do with aught of high or vast,
With havocs, wars, or towers, or a sphere
Splashing the west with silver as with foam?
For some old littleness would we clutch fast,
A shred of some lost crop, and clutching, hear
The sound of footsteps running back to home.

CALE YOUNG RICE

Author of twenty-three books of poems and four of prose, Cale Young Rice led a life of constant literary activity. He was born in Dixon, Kentucky, December 7, 1872, and was the recipient of degrees from Cumberland University, Harvard, Rollins College, and the University of Louisville. In 1902 he married Alice Caldwell Hegan (Alice Hegan Rice), the celebrated author of *Mrs. Wiggs of the Cabbage Patch*. Mr. Rice's death in January, 1943, has deprived us not only of a talented writer of songs but of one of our few noteworthy creators of plays in verse. His posthumous collection, *The Best Poetic Work of Cale Young Rice*—from which the following pieces are culled—was issued in 1943.

THE MYSTIC

There is a quest that calls me,
   In nights when I am lone,
The need to ride where the ways divide
   The Known from the Unknown.
I mount what thought is near me
   And soon I reach the place,
The tenuous rim where the Seen grows dim
   And the Sightless hides its face.

I have ridden the wind,
I have ridden the sea,
I have ridden the moon and stars.
I have set my feet in the stirrup seat
Of a comet coursing Mars.
And everywhere
Through the earth and air
My thought speeds, lightning-shod,
It comes to a place where checking pace
It cries, 'Beyond lies God!'

It calls me out of the darkness,
  It calls me out of sleep,
'Ride! Ride! for you must, to the end of Dust!'
  It bids—and on I sweep
To the wide outposts of Being,
  Where there is Gulf alone—
And through a Vast that was never passed
  I listen for Life's tone.

I have ridden the wind,
I have ridden the night,
I have ridden the ghosts that flee
From the vaults of death like a chilling breath
Over eternity.
And everywhere
Is the world laid bare—
Ether and star and clod—
Until I wind to its brink and find
But the cry, 'Beyond lies God!'

It calls and ever calls me!
  And vainly I reply,
'Fools only ride where the ways divide
  What Is from the Whence and Why!'
I am lifted into the saddle
  Of thoughts too strong to tame,
And down the deeps and over the steeps
  I find . . . ever the Same.

I have ridden the wind,
I have ridden the stars,
I have ridden the force that flies
With far intent through the firmament
And each to each allies.
And everywhere

That a thought may dare
To gallop, mine has trod—
Only to stand at last on the strand
Where just beyond lies God.

DUSK FROM A TRAIN WINDOW

There is a moment between day and night
When magic lives in light,
When snow upon the fields lies like blue sleep,
And the purple intricate trees
Stand out enchanted in the cold silences
Like branching mysteries;
A moment when one farm-lamp's window glow
Seems as I pass upon a speeding train
To make all human loss a sudden gain,
Because the ancient sacraments of home,
The humble sacraments of food and rest,
Are taken there in the untroubled gloam
By hearts that love, the ministrant, has blest.
There is a moment between day and night
When magic lives in light.

THE SOUND OF RAIN

Older than anything else in the world
Is the sound of rain.
Earth's without form again, and void,
And the waters cover it.
Land has not risen above its tidal plain,
And grey is the gloom of all, in and around and above it.

Life is an unborn brooding still
On the face of the earth,
And God has not found a way, yet,
To dwell in the waters.

And the sound of rain is a sound that is never still,
And men have not come yet, nor the sons of men nor the
　　daughters.

No green thing is about; and no bird's wing
Alights in branches.
Time and space are steeped in a sound
That is steeped in sorrow.
Winds are unknown; there is only room for the sigh
That besogs the day and the night, and the end of night, and
　　the morrow.

MARGARET R. RICHTER

Margaret R. Richter, a native of Ohio but a resident of
Los Angeles, has been successively a librarian and a uni-
versity instructor in English. Her poems have appeared
in various magazines and newspapers, and in thirty-two
anthologies. She received second prize in the Lola Ridge
Memorial Award contest in 1943; she was a contributing
editor of *The Spinners,* and editor of the California section
of Henry Harrison's *North America Book of Verse;* and is at
present poetry editor and columnist for *The Matrix,* a maga-
zine for women in journalism published by the Theta Sigma
Phi professional journalistic sorority.

GREEK VASE

Unplumbed the wellhead of this pantomime,
Rewarding still the unknown potter's toil;
Empty, this ewer pours forth very time
Instead of wine or oil:

Time that is gone and yet not passed away;
Time of the grave youth playing on his lyre,

Leaf-crowned, one unforgotten Grecian day,
Held in those lines, entire.

Through that one hour, remote to-day may peer
Upon the poet and the listening boy,
Knowing a far-off intimacy near,
Sharing their spell-bound joy.

Rapt in each other are they two, alone;
The fox-nosed dog unnoted sniffs a heel,
Before the moment and the song are blown
Down where the dead leaves reel.

UNBOWED

When life and matter keep their ancient tryst,
An oak has power to break the granite block;
No dead agglomeration can resist
The gnarled and growing tree within the rock—
A giant colony of cell on cell,
Sprung from one cell that split and split again,
Moved by the mystery that could compel
The endless struggle of the endless chain.
So even toadstools waxing underfoot
Deliberately toward air and sunshine plod,
With each day gaining strength enough to put
Aside the heavy covering of clod,
Till sturdier grown with each recurring strife
From earth is thrust the unbowed head of life.

CAROL M. RITCHIE

Carol M. Ritchie was educated in New York and Massachusetts, and now resides in Cambridge, in the latter state.

She is a contributor to the magazines; author of *Rhymer by Chance*, a book of poems; and a reviewer of books of poetry for the *Boston Herald* and the *Boston Traveler*.

HARVEST OF DUST

Rip up the sagebrush
That holds down the sand,
Turn the earth over,
Who cares for the land?
(Or that leaves should wither and roots should dry,
And the dust should choke and the cattle die.)

Keep on ploughing
For heavier yield,
Steely sun glaring
On desolate field.

(And a wind goes stirring the dusty plain
Till the dark clouds rise . . . but they are not rain.)

Furious, faster,
Go sowing the wheat,
What does it matter
So long as we eat?

(But the only harvest—and harsh winds sigh—
Is the phantom dust that goes whirling by.)

JESSIE B. RITTENHOUSE

One of the most distinguished names in contemporary American poetry is that of Jessie B. Rittenhouse. Her claim to recognition rests not only upon her accomplished creative work, but upon her pioneering service in the cause of modern poets and poetry, upon her lectures and critical activities, upon the series of notable anthologies which she edited, upon her attainments as the chief founder and for ten years the Secretary of the Poetry Society of America, and upon her establishment twenty years ago of the Poetry Society of Florida, of which she has been continuous President. A bronze medal for distinguished service to poetry has been awarded to Miss Rittenhouse by the Poetry Society of America, and her book *The Moving Tide* was voted a Poetry Week gold medal. A resident of Winter Park, Florida, Miss Rittenhouse was the wife of the well-known poet Clinton Scollard, who died in 1932 and whose selected poems she edited in 1934.

MY FATHER

My father was a tall man, and yet the ripened rye
Would come above his shoulders, the spears shot up so high.

My father was a tall man, and yet the tasselled corn
Would hide him when he cut the stalks upon a frosty morn.

The green things grew so lushly in the valley of my birth,
Where else could one so witness the luxuriance of earth?

The plow would turn so rhythmically the loose unfettered
    loam,
There was no need of effort to drive the coulter home.

My father walked behind his team before the sun was high,
Fine as a figure on a frieze cut sharp against the sky;

And when he swung the cradle in the yellow of the grain,
He could command all eyes around, or when he drove the
    wain.

I wonder if the acres now that lie so far away
Are waiting for his footprint at the coming of the day;

I wonder if the brown old barn that still is standing long
And ghostly cattle in the stalls are waiting for his song.

SOME STAR WITHIN ORION

The time approaches when I said good-bye
To you, more dear than ever one was dear.
It was the sad withdrawal of the year,
And many migrant wings were in the sky;
And when your life exhaled into a sigh,
With all the frosty heavens shining clear
And myriad worlds alluring, sphere on sphere—
How could I know to which your soul would fly?

But since you ever loved Orion best
Of all the wandering galaxies that roam,
And sang Orion ranging down the west
Or hanging low beneath the southern dome—
I dream when you essayed the final quest,
Some star within Orion called you home.

UNTO THE END

(To C. S.)

"I've known a cherry tree to blossom full
The year it died," my gardener said to me,
Not knowing that his simple words conveyed
The heart of poetry;

For your life blossomed full the year you died,
As mortal men know death,
Still putting forth its rich and joyous hope
Until the final breath.

THE NIGHTINGALES OF SURREY

The nightingales of Surrey
They hear the planes go by,
Yet fling upon the evening air
Their sharp, ecstatic cry.

God gave the creatures joy of life,
Joy of the perfect law,
While man reverts to jungle days
Of tooth and claw.

GRACE MARGARET ROBERTSON

Grace Margaret Robertson, at present a resident of Swampscott, Massachusetts, began writing poetry "in earnest" about 1934, "just as a means of self-expression." She has appeared in many of the verse magazines, and has won a number of prizes, including the *American Weave* brochure publication award for 1943.

ALL IS HIDDEN, NAUGHT CONCEALED

The cakes I have eaten, the wine I have drunk, and the lips
I have kissed
Have become as a dream, are dissolved into infinite mist;
And the things that are ended, the numberless hours of the
past
Have yielded their substance, have come to a reckoning at
last.

In the shade of the candle, the light of the moon, or the leap
of the flame,
Each mood is unmasked, and each mystery given a name;

From the prison of silence, no word and no thought shall
    escape
Though nightlong the shadows of sentries may gibber and
    gape.

Long lost to the vision, and far from the memory of man,
The world, which has grown to a bubble for bursting,
    began;
Though it last till he creep to the edge of the outermost sun,
Not a word has been lost, not a sum in addition is done.

ALBERTA ROBISON

Alberta Robison was born in Council Bluffs, Iowa; was
brought to California at the age of one year; and graduated
from the College of the Pacific in 1927. She lives in Los
Angeles, and is the author of one brochure of lyrics, entitled
modestly *Poems.*

STATUS

Half I belong with those who toil and half with those who
    sing,
With those who bend the burdened back, and those who
    spread the wing,
With those who, balked and baffled, still stumble sorely on,
And those who glide with easy grace into the golden dawn.

Half I belong with those who weep and half with those
    who smile,
With those who blindly grope the inch, and those who leap
    the mile,
Half, skeptical of any gain, half, certain past all doubt
That though woe enters early, yet joy will see him out.

E. MERRILL ROOT

E. Merrill Root, a native of Baltimore, is Professor of English at Earlham College, Indiana, one of the three leading Friends' colleges in the country. He has been, at various times, an editor of *The Measure* and *The Poetry Folio;* has contributed poems, reviews and articles to periodicals such as the *American Mercury, Forum, Commonweal, Christian Century,* etc., and has appeared in some of the best-known anthologies; has lectured extensively; and has issued three books of poetry and one of prose. His work has been acclaimed by critics as diverse as Frank Harris and Robert Frost.

PHOENIX

I heard men cry, "The sun shall die
  And the children of the sun!
Blossom and bird, and deed and word,
  Are the foam of oblivion.

"Fire's passion shall cease in the dark that is peace,
  And wolf and war shall end;
The flesh shall forget the blood's red fret,
  And foe shall be merged in friend.

"The moons that are white with the echo of light
  Shall end in a blackened arc;
Each earth shall die in a sunless sky,
  And none shall say 'See!' or 'Hark!'

"Back to the tomb of the primal womb
  And the slumber of ancient death
Go cloud and stream, and song and dream,
  And the fruitful gasp of breath.

"The rainbow's dome has the sun for home—
　　The colors shall die with the light;
The seasons tossed between fire and frost
　　Shall end in the equal night.

"His destiny done, the fierce blond sun
　　Shall be black and brittle bone;
His every planet shall freeze to granite
　　And the seas to a crystal stone.

"The eagles of light that harry the night,—
　　Arcturus, Antares,—then
Shall feel their golden unrest unfolden
　　In the calm of night again.

"All woes and joys shall find equipoise:
　　The dream and the deed be one:
The mane and the fleece lie down in peace:
　　And Time be a skeleton.

"Therefore secure we can endure
　　To battle with wind and wave;
Beyond the toss of gain and loss
　　Lies the dark wharf of the grave.

"The Child of the Light and the Child of the Night
　　Both find what the one foresees:
Over all the sky the day shall die
　　In the night of the primal ease!"

Unmoved I heard their prophecy's word,
　　Though myself I worship the sun:
O word uncouth with the half of truth—
　　That the deed, being done, is done!

I too foresee the victory
　　Of the night concluding the flame;

I do not doubt that the suns go out
  In the darkness—whence they came.

Yet I know that they burst from chaos at first
  When all was wingless night;
And how have faith in the power of death
  That is only the shell of light?

O eagles that broke from the night's dull yolk
  In a first wild miracle,
Wake, wake, once more to flutter and soar
  Like fiery birds from the shell!

FLORENCE WILSON ROPER

Florence Wilson Roper, who was born in Richmond, Virginia, in 1882, but has lived in Petersburg in the same state ever since her marriage in 1900, is the winner of many poetic awards: the Kaleidograph Book Publication prize in 1932, the *Commonwealth* award, and the poetry prize of the Virginia Federated Women's Clubs. She is a contributor to the magazines and the author of two books, which reveal her as a writer of accomplished technique and of unusual strength and sweep of thought and feeling.

THIS MUCH I KNOW

This much I know of life: Nothing is sure
But time in its unalterable flight,
Nor joy, nor any grief, that will endure
Beyond a night.

This much I know of love: We may not eat
The dainty viands spread and have them too—

But, ah, my friends, the taste is very sweet
The banquet through.

This much I know of death: Its arms are strong,
And there, bewildered, drowsily we creep,
And gently, very gently, dream and song
Are hushed to sleep.

THE OCEAN

What if my vision shows a curving pond
Outlined in feathery scallopings of lace?
I know the ocean stretches leagues beyond,
An unperturbed immensity of space.
What matter if my finite eyes can see
But one white sail against the glowing west,
I know with all a dreamer's certainty
She wears a thousand ships upon her breast;
I know ten thousand times ten thousand years
Before the eyes of men watched from the dune,
Radiant with hope, or blinded by their tears,
Her silver tides were bridled by the moon.
So dare I vision life—a glimpse of sea—
An edge of spray—beyond, infinity.

IF THERE IS THOUGHT AMONG THE DAFFODILS

If there is Thought among the daffodils,
And Wisdom in the humble daisy fields,
And all the white-starred dust the hawthorn spills,
And every buttercup that summer yields;
Who stand in beauty, laughter in their eyes,
Their little feet deep-rooted in the ground,
If they have learned from dust how to be wise,
And how from death the voice of Truth to sound,
Then we, who strangely come and strangely go,
And stalk our food throughout a sunless day,

Who ever question and yet never know.
Walking like shadows through a mist of gray,
With joy and thankful hearts may welcome death,
Who finds all knowledge on a flower's breath!

FLAME AGAINST THE WIND

Within myself, this bit of dying dust
That time each day with sure precision mars,
Beneath the slow corrode, the creeping rust,
A something lives that contemplates the stars.
Beyond the glitter of the cradled throng,
Within myself, a watcher of the sky
Has wrung from distant harmonies of song
One broken chord to measure Heaven by.
A flame against the wind, serene, aloof,
It dares to burn across the darkest night,
As constellations in the vaulted roof
Of heaven blaze, immutable with light.
A flame beyond the reach of dying clod,
Within myself, omnipotent, is God!

God in his Heaven—whirling with his hand
The universes in their destined place,
God in the heart that dares to understand,
God in the mind that never sees his face.
God in the grass, the flower, the leaf, the tree,
The full corn in the ear, the quickening seed,
God in the wind, the earth, the sky, the sea,
In every stick and stone and dusty weed,
God in the song that ripples from the breast
Of each gay-plumaged bird with trilling note,
God in the humble sparrow in her nest
Though dumb the song within her muted throat.
God in myself, the living vital part,
His soul the dream that flames within my heart.

SYDNEY KING RUSSELL

An editor of *Poetry Chap-book*, a former associate editor
of *Voices*, and the author of seven books of verse, Sydney
King Russell is known wherever American poets congregate.
His work, which is predominantly of a lyrical nature, has
appeared in many anthologies, including those of Moult and
Braithwaite and the *New Yorker Book of Verse;* he has con-
tributed recently to the *American Mercury* and numerous
other magazines. Early in 1945 he won the W. W. Kimball
award of $100 for a prize song. For a number of years he
lived in Southern California, but at present he is in New
York.

AFTER HOUR

This is the hardest hour of all to bear,
When I turn slowly back to my still room
Where have you been, who are no longer there—
This is the after hour, when shadows loom
And walls bend down to listen, when delight
Is lost in doubt, and dark forebodings press
Upon the uneasy heart, when all the night
Is heavy with the weight of loneliness.

This room has known you—table, hearth and chair
Treasured your chiming laughter. Now the spell
Is shattered by the closing of a door.
This is the darkest hour of all to bear
Alone in my still room that knew you well
And loving you, will know you now no more.

VACHEL LINDSAY

So many songs he had to sing
He knew no time to gather bread,

And April found him wandering
Without a place to lay his head.

Death saw no terror in his face—
So many songs he had to spare
That Heaven is now a merry place
And he a welcome comrade there.

PRAYER

Let me remember music
When music is no more
Than the far beat of breakers
Upon a windy shore.

Though sorrow cast his shadow
And tears of anguish flow,
Let me remember music
From long and long ago.

Though laughter may be muted
And mournful eyelids wet,
Let me remember music
The heart must not forget,

Lest in the dark forgetting
In seasons of unrest
The lonely heart should perish
Within the stricken breast.

ARCHIBALD RUTLEDGE

Archibald Rutledge was born in 1883 in McClellanville,
South Carolina, which is still his home. He is the author of

a number of books in prose and verse, as well as of magazine
articles; several years ago he was made poet laureate of his
native state by decree of the legislature.

THE VEERY

When day is hushed and hidden,
And golden woods are mute,
The Elegist of Evening
Touches a silver lute—

As if through lonely oriels
Of sundown's gorgeous fane
Resplendent dying beauty sang
Anthems of love and pain;

As if the light were lyric
That from the first star gleams,
Far through the dewy pinewood
The glimmering choral streams;

As if a rosebay's beauty
In music overbrimmed,
Till all the fading forest hears
Her radiant vespers hymned;

As if a heart long harried,
And scourged by many a rod,
Had triumphed, and were singing
Safe in the arms of God.

ARTHUR WILLIAM RYDER

The tall, virile figure of Arthur William Ryder was for
years a familiar figure on the campus of the University of

California at Berkeley. A most unprofessorial professor, who cared more for philosophy and poetry than for scholasticism, he was known to a far wider audience than his immediate college circle. He was celebrated for his translations of the *Bhagavad-gita,* the *Panchatantra, The Ten Princes,* and other Hindu classics, and his work as a translator has been declared by one of his colleagues, G. R. Noyes, to be on the whole "probably the finest ever accomplished by an American." Yet he has also some original poems that show the bent of his unique and brilliant personality.

Arthur William Ryder was born in Oberlin, Ohio, in 1877, and died in March 1938, of a heart attack that overtook him while he was teaching.

AËTIUS AT CHALONS, SEPTEMBER, 451

Yes, I have crushed them; yet a few more years
The empire staggers, free from sickening fears
Lest all the glory of its massive past,
Dishonored now, decaying to the last,
    By vermin Hun,
    Poisoned, undone,
Should rot in death irreparably vast.

Nay, heaven could not decree that such a foe
Should win, that Caesar's Rome should perish so—
By witches' seed struck down, with black, lank hair,
Whom devils fathered in a desert lair,
    Their cheeks rough-gashed,
    Their noses pashed,
Moon-legs, and deep-slit eyes with lust aglare.

Yet why these labors for a dying state?
Why struggle briefly for a certain fate?
Why strive to keep the body still upright
When that is gone for which men love to fight?

For well I know
The Gothic woe
Engulfs the world, and superstitious night.

The Gothic and Germanic brotherhood
We hate, as always, both for ill and good;
Though all are brave and many of them chaste,
By vulgar vice each virtue is defaced;
    Their brutal, rude
    Dull hardihood
Creeps low, by stern, artistic aim ungraced.

And they inherit man's great centuries—
The sombre dignity of Rameses,
Plato's clear light that calms us while it thrills,
And Caesar's splendid majesty, that fills
    The trump of time
    With breath sublime,
From Nile re-echoing to the Roman hills.

Dark days I see, when faith and grace are gone
And art that warms a man to look upon,
When Christian superstition onward creeps,
Obliterating human depths and steeps,
    When honor's prize
    With honor dies,
When priests and women rule, for manhood sleeps.

Religion is like empire; they alone
Are fit to keep it who create their own;
While worship borrowed from a foreign sky
Serves only to deceive and stupefy
    (For tyrants' use
    And priests' abuse)
Brave men, and at the last will surely die.

So is my question answered; I must fight
Just to abridge the inevitable night;
To bring some civilizing vision home
To these rough German brutes, of what was Rome,
    That they may see
    The mystery,
Ere all dissolve in froth and bloody foam.

What will the world be, when at last the dawn
Kindles, the sadness of the night is gone?
Decaying Egypt could not well foresee
What Greece, decaying Greece what Rome should be;
    And sudden change
    As great as strange,
Will startle men again and make them free.

In this assured belief I fight forlorn
For men whose parents' parents are unborn;
For men who never will be told that I
(And some few others) did not weakly cry,
    But conquering fears
    Shed blood for tears
And dared to fight unthanked, unpaid to die.

Arthur M. Sampley

Arthur M. Sampley has been in the past few years a Professor of English and a first lieutenant in the Army Air Forces, and is now Director of Libraries at North Texas State Teachers College. His sonnet sequence *Fragments of Eternity* won the award in a national contest conducted in 1937 by *Wings, A Quarterly of Verse;* he has won three major awards of the Poetry Society of Texas; and was co-winner in 1939 of the Maxwell Anderson Award in Verse Drama offered by Stanford University. His verse has appeared in *Yearbooks* of the Poetry Society of Texas, *New York Times*, *Saturday Review of Literature*, and other periodicals. He is the author of two books of verse.

FROM *FRAGMENTS OF ETERNITY*

I

THE DEAD EARTH

The dark, dim centuries at last shall cease,
And time, like some worn clock, run down and die.
Then this black coal wrapped in eternal peace
Will wander tenantless along the sky.
There then will be no memory of the bright,
Sweet, happy hours we two together sped,
Nor will young lovers in their flame's clear light
See shadows of ourselves long past and dead.
When the dark oceans wash on ghostly shores
With never a sail to break the plangent main,
There will be no faint music in their roars
To pulse to rhythms of some sad lover's pain.
What voices dead, what tasks forever done
Beneath the bleak, cold rays of that last sun!

II

ETERNITY

There will be roses after you are gone;
There will be maidens plucking them to wear;
Above your silent grave the crimson dawn
Will shoot bright streamers through the morning air.
Love will be wandering down the aisles of June,
And many a sigh and many a tender pain

In lovers' breasts will beat a fairy tune
When no faint memories of you remain.
But let the beauty die, the glory fade,
For care will stain, and time, O love, will rust:
The incandescent sun shall turn to shade,
And the eternal marble ruin to dust.
Yet in your beauty's poignant mystery,
As in her godhead, lives Eternity.

CLINTON SCOLLARD

"He had such joy in nature, such love for every phase of beauty that, wherever he went, he brought back a song." So writes the poet and anthologist Jessie B. Rittenhouse, the wife of Clinton Scollard, in her feeling introduction to Scollard's posthumous selected poems, *The Singing Heart—* poems that amply testify to the truth of this remark.

During the years preceding Scollard's death in 1932, one could hardly take up a magazine or a newspaper poetry column without expecting to see the name of this prolific writer. Throughout a long life he was faithful to his muse, turning out books of verse innumerable, all of them transfused with the element of song. He was born in Clinton, New York, September 18, 1860; was educated at Hamilton College, where he afterwards was Associate Professor of English; traveled extensively abroad; and was the author of a number of successful novels, but in 1912 decided to abandon fiction in favor of his true love, poetry.

AN AUTUMN CRICKET

In the warm hush of the autumnal night
I hear one lonely cricket sound its clear
Persistent music, telling that the year

Has passed the summer zenith of delight.
And though I know that soon in gypsy flight
The birds will wing, and all the hills grow drear,
Yet does my heart keep constant hold on cheer,
Harkening this tiny minstrel-eremite.

Then keep your fine-keyed instrument in tune
O small musician, till the last leaf falls
And the last blossom shrivels with the rime,
That I may stray through Autumn's ruined halls
With golden memories for a buoy and boon,
Indifferent to the onward tread of Time!

HARDING HILL

In Kirkland glen the snows are deep;
By Ely Brook no wanderer goes;
White as the new-washed fleece of sheep
The Post Street ways are lost in snows;
And the great north wind trumpets shrill
Amid the woods on Harding Hill.

I tarry lonely leagues afar
From these familiar scenes of white,
But here no sun, no vesper star—
A beacon on the marge of night—
Sheds fairer beams than those that fill
With light the woods on Harding Hill.

I hear the low-winged meadow-lark
Its limpid, liquid strain prolong;
Until the closing in of dark
I catch the echo of its song;
It bears me back: I hear the trill
Of thrushes upon Harding Hill.

So though I know the clutch of cold
Is rigid where the maples stand,
I am the boy who strayed of old
Along the rising valley land,
On summer twilights cool and still
Beneath the woods on Harding Hill.

ONE SONG MORE

Just one song more, then the long sleep and silence;
Just one song more, and then the set of sun;
Just one song more, and then the shrouding darkness,
With the long journey done.

Ah, who can say when we shall reawaken,
If short shall be our slumbering or long?
Happy were we to know that our arising
Would be to some glad song!

THE SLEEPER

Above the cloistral valley,
Above the druid rill,
There lies a quiet sleeper
Upon a lonely hill.

All the long days of summer
The low winds whisper by,
And the soft voices of the leaves
Make murmurous reply.

All the long eves of autumn
The loving shadows mass
Round this sequestered slumbering-place
Beneath the cool hill grass.

All the long nights of winter
The white drifts heap and heap
To form a fleecy coverlet
Above the dreamer's sleep.

Ah, who would break the rapture,
Brooding and sweet and still,
The great peace of the sleeper
Upon the lonely hill!

RUBY T. SCOTT

Ruby T. Scott is a professor in the English Department of the University of Toledo, and the contributor of occasional poems to the magazines.

MUSEUM METEORITE

Neatly labeled, it lies at last
A lump of iron and stone,
Whirled out of loneliness more vast
Than any man has known.

Whence came this iron adventurer?
From what portentous sire
This energy-made Lucifer,
This sibling born of fire?

Molten in heat too fierce for flame,
Through interstellar space
And zero's ultimate it came—
Here to this quiet place.

Pulled out of darkness, burned in air,
Flashing across the skies,

Light-years lost in the otherwhere,
Motionless now it lies

Dull and inert on a dusty shelf
For any man to see:
For any man—who is himself
No less a mystery.

ANDERSON M. SCRUGGS

It would be impossible to read much current American magazine verse without encountering the work of Anderson M. Scruggs, a contributor to many of the best-known periodicals as well as to a number of anthologies. He is the author of two books, *Glory of Earth* (Oglethorpe University Press) and *Ritual for Myself* (Macmillan), both of which show him as a convinced traditionalist, with a considerable command of expression and a deep sensitiveness to nature.

Born in West Point, Georgia, in 1897, Mr. Scruggs occupies a position such as, certainly, few poets have ever attained, that of Professor of Histology in the Emory University School of Dentistry.

SONG FOR DARK DAYS

He is an alien to all grief whose heart
Has learned the wisdom hills and woodlands know;
The plundering hands of men can never part
Peace from still leaves or silence from the snow.
The gathering tumult of the centuries,
Strident with greed and loud with human toil,
More lightly falls than twilight on these trees,
More softly than cloud shadows on this soil.

Time trails no wings of anguish when the mind
Can lose its sorrow in a wind's caress;
Who seeks the voice of streams will never find
Strife in his bosom, and whose footfalls press
The soft, warm turf upon a winter's day
May sense a peace beyond the flesh's knowing.
No greed of man can turn one wind away,
No Armageddon stop one rose's blowing.

Then let the dark days come, the little ills
That twitch the flesh, the rancor and the dearth;
There yet remains the heritage of hills,
The old, old dream incumbent in the earth.
The noisy hordes of men go clattering by,
But fields lie deep in silence as they pass;
The olden beauty hovers in the sky,
The ancient glory lingers in the grass.

GLORY TO THEM

Glory to them, the toilers of the earth,
Who wrought with knotted hands, in wood and stone,
Dreams their unlettered minds could not give birth
And symmetries their souls had never known.
Glory to them, the artisans, who spread
Cathedrals like brown lace before the sun,
Who could not build a rhyme, but reared instead
The Doric grandeur of the Parthenon!

I never cross a marble portico,
Or lift my eyes where stained glass windows steal
From virgin sunlight moods of deeper glow,
Or walk dream-peopled streets except to feel
A hush of reverence for that vast dead
Who gave us beauty for a crust of bread.

KARL SHAPIRO

Karl Shapiro, one of the most widely commended of the younger poets, is at present with the United States armed forces in the South Pacific. His book, *V-Letter and Other Poems*, won a Pulitzer Prize in 1944.

ON READING KEATS IN WARTIME

As one long lost in no-man's-land of war
Dreams of a cup of pure forgetful wine,
Dark waters deeper than the ancient Rhine
Where Saturnalian maidens swam before
The age of knowledge, and all your golden lore
Held in the splendor of a castle's shine
At sunset on a crag of somber pine—
But wakes to death and thirst and cannon's roar;

So I have come upon your book and drunk
Even to the dregs of melancholy bliss
Your poetry, Keats, and smoothing down your page,
Thought how a soldier leaner than a monk
Still loves, though time without the lover's kiss
Pours out its viscous hemlock on our age.

GRACE BUCHANAN SHERWOOD

Grace Buchanan Sherwood, of Garden City, Long Island, was born in New York in 1893, and graduated from the Spence School in 1904. She is the author of various magazine verses, and of five collections of poems, the latest being *No Final Breath* (1940).

NOW WALKS THE DEVIL UP AND DOWN

Now walks the Devil up and down
This apprehensive world;
The masque has slipped that held his frown,
His dark flag streams unfurled.

Yet all across the countryside
The light becomes a thing
More precious than before black pride
Swept down its stormy wing.

Though hate's mad image stalks abroad,
These airs are grown more dear;
And special fragrances are poured
From trees, in spite of fear.

Now is the time to emulate
This light, these airs and trees;
Pure beauty, held inviolate,
Belongs to days like these.

Forget to paint the ugly thing;
Remember ancient grace;
Oh, now, if ever, you that sing,
Bring hope from music's face.

CLARK ASHTON SMITH

"For what is called 'pure' poetry, one shall search for his equal in vain among contemporary poets," wrote George Sterling many years ago of Clark Ashton Smith. Mr. Smith, a protégé of Sterling, is the author of four books of verse, some of which flared into such prominence more than two decades ago that today they are collectors' items. He was born in 1893 in Long Valley, California, and lives by himself in a cabin at Auburn, from which he issues his imaginative and original and often singularly fantastic poems, and his stories of the "weird" or "occult" genre, of which two volumes have recently been published. His poetry and fiction have appeared in more than fifty magazines, including the *Yale Review, London Mercury, Asia,* etc.

TOWN LIGHTS

To him who wanders up and down
Its long-familiar streets in autumn nights
With melancholy meaning shine the lights
Of the small, scattered town.

Often, where lamp-bright windows cast
Their homely splendor forth on tree and lawn,
Strange moths of dream and memory are drawn,
Flown from the ghostly past.

And kisses faint as falling mist
Await the wanderer at some old door,
And sorrowful voices crying Nevermore
From bygone lips he left unkissed.

What panes illumed by love's own lamp
Are darkened now, or lit by alien hands;
Where friendship sat before the rose-red brands
Comes in the invasive cold and damp,

Or strangers make oblivious cheer:
Till he who watches dimly from without
Feels as a leaf blown in the autumn's rout
From desolate trees foredoomed and sere.

But still he turns, and marks again
Some aureate lamp that friends have lit afar;
Some radiance, with love for inner star,
That burns behind a trellised pane;

Knowing if it were not for these
His vagrant soul would haunt a homeless night,
Even as an exile phantom, borne in flight
Past unapproachable galaxies.

STRANGE GIRL

What bond was this, of life or doom,
That swiftly drew your eyes to mine
Beyond the drinkers and the wine,
Across the crowded, garish room?

Beauty was yours, but beauty lost,
Bringing to that familiar bar
The luster of a fallen star
On strands of night and chaos tossed.

O yours were soft, unhappy lips,
O yours were hard, unhappy eyes,
Like agates under glacial skies
Laden with tempest and eclipse.

Upon the delicate chin you turned
Venus had set her cloven sign.
Like embers seen through darkest wine
Your unextinguished tresses burned.

Your gown revealed that gracious form
Tanagra's sculptors loved to mould
In clay immortal from of old,
With limbs forever sweet and warm.

Of what we spoke, it matters not:
For in your wistful voice I heard
What hidden things that found no word—
Broken, half-dreamed, or half-forgot.

Girlishly, half maternally,
You chid me for the fault we shared:
Your voice was sweet . . . your eyes despaired . . .
It was your eyes that wounded me,

So bleak they were, so wan and chill,
Like eyes that meet the Gorgon's gaze
Amid the untraversable maze
Of all-reverting shame and ill.

But when you leaned to kiss me there,
It seemed some fragile moth of night
Had softly touched my lips in flight,
Swerving athwart the untroubled air.

Sister you seemed to all the woe
My heart has known but never sung. . . .
Was it for this your fingers clung
To mine, as loath to let me go?

THE HILL-TOP

Alone upon my hill-top
After the trailing rains,
I see the cloudy mountains,
I see the misty plains.

Fair is my hill, and rugged,
Where silken grasses grow,
And the drifted clouds go by me
More soft than woven snow.

The pale fantastic lichens
Make patterns on the stone,
And the oaks are old and dwarfèd,
With golden mosses grown.

Beneath the ancient boulders
There dwells the shadowy fern;
And here the twisted pine-trees
To shapes of beauty turn.

I wander through the seasons
And mix my thoughts unknown
With the little flowers of springtime,
With the leaves of autumn flown.

Between the plains and the mountains,
Between the clouds and the grass,
I find the dreams that linger,
And the fairer dreams that pass.

RICHARD LEON SPAIN

Richard Leon Spain was born in 1916 in Mangum, Oklahoma, and has lived much of his life in the Arkansas Ozarks. He began writing poetry at the age of twelve, and his work has subsequently appeared in more than seventy-five periodicals in the United States and England; his *Arkansas Poems* won honorable mention in 1935 in the annual contest of *Poetry*. His work has an authentic quality, and in particular a genuineness of reaction to nature, which has justified a number of well-known critics in commending him as one of the most promising of the younger poets. *Rock and Cumulus*, his first book, was published in 1942 by the League to Support Poetry.

EASTER ISLAND

There is an island in the warm Pacific
Inhabited by towering carved stone faces
From some forgotten time; there are no traces
Of whose they were—not tool or hieroglyphic.
Were they fierce men, those sculptors? Did they come
In swift canoes to war along the reef?
I wonder on their love, their mirth, their grief;
And did they dance—by flames—to pipe or drum?
What race was this, in what deep century,
That Time has swept—as with omnivorous broom—
All their identity away, and bars
Our baffled hands from the bright, ultimate key—
That only these gaunt crumbling faces loom
Lonely and terrible against the stars?

AT TIMBERLINE

Here is the high arena of the winds
Between wild crags that shoulder to the blue,
A cold clear height where only rock ascends,
In the old way, unchanged since earth was new.

Here is the steep where blooms no tender flower,
The silence that no earthly bird dares break—
Charged with the Absolute in awful power,
Forever still, eternally awake;

And here the bent tree grows, aloof, alone
From a seed spilled in some forgotten year—
Torn derelict above—sure root in stone—
The one green shard of life that braves the austere.

Give me this eminence from which to see
The bright-veined storms upon a distant hill,

Spending their futile rage and far from me
While my brief world stands high and clear and still;

And in this place where calm and tumult part
My parting with old grief will be as sure;
I shall know peace—not wordless in the heart
But carved in mountain granite to endure.

EVENING BY THE SEA: THE PLOVERS FLY

When evening winds, with ghostly violining,
Play on the shoreline trees, then from afar
The plovers come, whose wings are made for seaways,
Skimming the sand-dune's long light-studded bar.
Silent and swift they dart, the weaving flock,
Past yellow ruffles and deep purple spaces
Wind-fluted, wave-embossed along the beach
Where blue mist flowers and the swift tide races.

Into the sun they turn with soft, quick calling,
And light glints golden on their storm-stained breasts,
Wild, with the hearts like sea-beat in them, tracing
In flight the swerve and fumble of the crests.
Into the infinite maze they dip and settle,
Rise and cut nimbly through the branching spray—
They that adore the winds' and breakers' singing,
Follow until the last sun laps away.

Then the blue dusk sheathes down the saffron sky
And for an instant-space the waves loom tall,
Poised, sculptured, rose and mauve and indigo
Before the thundering cascade of their fall.
And high across the west where flags of fire
Upon invisible masts are furled and swung
Like an immense and solitary flower
The evening star is hung.

Now I who watch, by some strange chemistry
Of thought, lose my identity with man;
No longer locked within one finite being,
Walled by the heart and mind's brief actual span,
I am for this enchanted interval
No more germane to joy and fear and grief
Than wave-struck rock or cloud or blowing wind.
I hear the rustle of a single leaf,
I hear the plovers, finished with their flight,
Sunk to their nests beyond the darkening dune;
And I, with them, am close a part of this
World of great shining sky and wheeling sea,
Part of eternity.

CAROLYN SPENCER

Carolyn Spencer, of Los Angeles, has been contributing poems for years to the verse magazines. The following shows her in one of her more emotional strains.

ALONE

Well I remember that bleak day of snow,
Of sullen skies and searching, angry winds—
How my stern father came and held me up,
Too small a child to see you as you lay;
How from the chill aloofness of your smile,
And from your form so strangely still I turned,
Half-comprehending, suddenly desolate,
And hid my face against his breast and yearned
For some belated hint of tenderness.
But coldly, as his way had ever been,
He but unclasped, slowly, my clinging arms

About his neck, and led me, shrinking, in
Among the funeral guests.

                         And even now
That early loss comes crying at my heart:
I stand again the timid, wistful child,
Bewildered, in my ugly dress of black,
Among the whispering neighbors, and I feel
Again the curious, prying eyes— And you . . .
In the long box . . . helpless to comfort me.

ANN STANFORD

Ann Stanford, of Los Angeles, is a native Californian, and
a graduate of Stanford University. She made her literary
debut in 1937 in the anthology *Twelve Poets of the Pacific;*
in 1938-39 she held a Phelan Fellowship in Literature; and
subsequently has contributed verse and prose to magazines
and anthologies, and has published one collection of poems,
In Narrow Bound (1943).

ON A SHIP AT SEA

We know not where horizons end:
Their slow progression gives the eye
Only a wave to mark them by.
In perfect orb the waters bend.

We are the center, and a world
Advances with us as we move.
With time and shore together furled
What is behind we cannot prove.

Below us, dark and peaceful now,
Deep over deep the cavern lies,
And nothing from its press can rise.
We see no deeper than the bow.

Our wake is lost this side the sky;
If waters cover us at last,
It will but for a moment lie
Tracing the way that we have passed.

Hold fast the star and compass then;
By their firm counsel we must find
The hill-walled harbor we designed,
The sureness to go forth again.

VICTOR STARBUCK

When Victor Starbuck died on March 31, 1935, he was vainly seeking a publisher for his *Saul, King of Israel,* a narrative poem which, despite its time-worn theme, flows with a martial sweep, a verve and variety of rhythm and an accomplished technique that should place it among the enduring epics of American literature. The book was published in 1938 by the University of North Carolina Press. The selections given below do not illustrate the rushing and colorful narrative passages, which are too long for quotation; but they will at least indicate the carefully molded quality of the whole.

Starbuck, who was born in Chuluota, Florida, in 1887 and later practiced law in Asheville, North Carolina, is the author of one previous book of verse, published by Yale University Press in 1923.

FROM *SAUL, KING OF ISRAEL*

JABESH GILEAD

Who hath despised the day of little things—
The baby at the breast, the child at play,
The colt with wind-tossed mane? Who shall misprize
The lion's whelp, the eagle's young, whose wings,
Half-fledged, are yet too feeble to essay
The sun's dominions and the realms of day?
He yet shall dare the winds and mount the skies,
And swoop, with rending talons, on the prey.
The warrior armed, the lion when he cries
Full-voiced, were feeble once: now who so strong as they?

And he that builds a realm must sweat and bleed
Through days of doubt and danger, laboring long,
While frost and wrinkle mar the cheek and hair,
And all his striving brings but scanty meed:
The mighty men despise him, and the throng
Beholds unheeding; but the man grows strong
Through failure and defeat, and learns to dare,
To judge, to rule, to overcome the wrong.
And in the end shall be the trumpet's blare,
The crown of victory, the harping and the song.

GILBOA

All things shall have an end: the more and less
  Contrived of men, the cities and the towers
  Are overturned by the unpitying hours,
And sown with ashes of forgetfulness.

Go, seek the kingdoms that were great of yore:
  For Noph lies waste, and Nineveh forgets;
  On Tyre's wet rocks the fishers spread their nets,
And Ilium is a memory by the shore.

Yea, ask of Gibeah, or ask of Gath!
  They now are resting places for the flocks;
  The conies hide among the tumbled rocks,
And Time hath swept their glories from his path.

And Saul and Achish—names by men forgot,
  Blurred characters in some old manuscript,
  Long hid and mouldering in a sunless crypt
O'er which the shepherd treads, and dreams it not.

Their trumps are silent and their standards furled;
  Their laurels have been withered by the gust;
  Their fiery hearts are crumbled into dust
To ride the winds that blow across the world.

Yet once their shouting shook the earth with dread;
  At their command would thousands gird the sword—
  Their chariots thundered and their trumpets roared,
And war's red harvest heaped the fields with dead.

VINCENT STARRETT

Vincent Starrett was born in Toronto, Canada, on October 26, 1886; and has served as a newspaper reporter in Chicago, and as a war correspondent in Mexico in 1914-15. He is well known as the author of nearly thirty volumes, many of them dealing with excursions among books. His home is in Chicago.

NOVEMBER 24, 1918

I died last night. . . . Upon a narrow bed
I saw my body sink to dreamless sleep.
The silence of the room was strange and deep:

A white nurse held my hand; no words were said,
Until one whispered "Gone!" . . . And I lay there,
Who but a moment since had breathed and sighed,
With the gray smile of one who just had died,
And the white nurse's fingers in my hair.

Thus died my father, brave and strong and true,
Loving life much, and laughter more than tears . . .
Listening now there rings within my ears
His deep, fine laugh, out of the utmost blue . . .
But in that dreadful moment by his side
It was my father's son that gasped and died.

MARGUERITE STEFFAN

Marguerite Steffan was born in Austria-Hungary, and
came to the United States in 1905. She obtained her A.B.
and M.A. degrees at the University of Georgia, and has made
her living teaching foreign languages; she is at present
Professor of French and German at Paine College. Her
poems have appeared in *Pictorial Review, New York Times,*
and other periodicals. She lives in Augusta, Georgia.

DANCE OF THE GNATS

What madly whirling universe is this,
What bacchanal of atoms drunk with light—
A sportive game, an amorous pursuit?
Embattled hosts, or weird religious rite?

Now constellations thicken to a clump,
Now spread in widening circles; there must be
A magnet nucleus, a central force
That holds all stragglers—winged, yet never free. . . .

So, as they wheel in ceaseless energy,
To ends unseen, around the selfsame place,
Perhaps, to vision without bounds, the suns
And planets too, are gnats that dance in space. . . .

THE NEGRO STUDENT

There is no latch on books, to say: "Stand back!
You dare not enter, for your skin is black!"
Here I tread boldly; take a foremost seat
Before a mighty stage, to hear the beat
Of man's heart through the ages; to unfold
The purple sails on Cydnus; to behold
The fall of Caesars. Here, my step grown free
In lofty halls resounding with the fame
Of those who saw, and toiled that all might see—
I, too, shall raise a pillar to my name!
Sweet chariot of free thought, you carry me
Beyond deep rivers turbid with the past.
To that high mountain, rising clear and blue,
Where mind of man shall pierce the fog at last,
And stand transfigured, daring to be true. . . .

GEORGE STERLING

One of the best-known poets ever to come out of the West,
and the author of some of the most consummate sonnets
and most graceful lyrics in American literature, George
Sterling was a protégé of Ambrose Bierce. He was born in
1869 in Sag Harbor, New York, but came to California early
in life. For many years his lean, esthetic-looking form was a
familiar sight among the woods and beaches of Carmel and
on the streets of San Francisco, where he lived at the cele-

brated Bohemian Club. It was there that, in 1926, he was found dead under circumstances pointing to suicide.

The best of Sterling's work is to be found in his *Selected Poems* (1923); yet his two posthumous volumes, *Sonnets to Craig* and *Poems to Vera*, while on the whole undoubtedly inferior, do occasionally rise to his most accomplished level, as in the examples given below.

LOVE'S SHADOW

Great love is ever sorrow. In some way
  I cannot picture but must always feel,
    Grief to great love is sacrament and seal—
On love's blue dome a distant cloud of grey;
A hush beyond the music of the day;
    A tabernacle pure where mourners kneel;
    A sunset fair on which the night shall steal;
Belovèd starlight that the dawn shall slay.

Ah! we who love, think not that we shall miss
  That sense of things too lovely to endure!
    For souls that know, as thine, his gracious lure,
    The seraph Sorrow hath his hidden skies,
And when I gain thy lips I somehow kiss
    That lonely angel of the solemn eyes.

AT THE GRAND CANYON

Thou settest splendors in my sight, O Lord!
  It seems as tho' a deep-hued sunset falls
    Forever on these Cyclopean walls,
These battlements where Titan hosts have warred,
And hewn the world with devastating sword,
    And shook with trumpets the eternal halls
    Where Seraphim lay hid by bloody palls
And only Hell and Silence were adored

Lo! the abyss wherein the wings of Death
Might beat unchallenged, and his fatal breath
 Fume up in pestilence. Beneath the sky
  Is no such testimony unto grief.
 Here Terror walks with Beauty ere she die.
  Oh! hasten to me, Love, for life is brief!

MYSTERY

 At times a breath
From out the distant Eden to be ours
  Wanders to me,
 And Love, defying Death,
Bends forth across the years to touch those flow'rs,
And trembles for the joy that is to be.

 At times the day
Is husht with all its voices, and I hear
  From thy far place
 Thy whisperings, that say
"Weep not! Put by thy sorrow and thy fear!
God's mercy yet shall bring us face to face!"

 At times the night
Seems holy with thy presence, and I feel,
  Soft on my brow,
 The wafture of thy flight—
Oh! on the paths of slumber dost thou steal
To find the heart that hungers for thee now?

MY SONGS

 Your beauty bids my spirit fare
  To heavens till now unknown;
 Earth's voices in that lyric air
  Sink to an undertone.

The world's hard truths are there a lie,
  Its joys are foolish things;
To those that gain the pathless sky
  Their sorrows are their wings.

Debarred (nor ever at my will)
  From that domain of blue,
Some echo of its music still
  I strive to hold for you—

The murmur of a song remote,
  Too faint for men to heed,
Yet dear to you because I wrote,
  To me because you read.

INCLUSION

I have heard music and the long wave falling,
  Where seas rejoice,
Wind in the trees and hidden thrushes calling:
  In all, thy voice!

I have seen jonquil-cups and weary roses,
  The lily's grace,
Faun-luring streams and stormy sunset-closes:
  In all, thy face!

I have had joy in pledges never spoken,
  In stars above,
In marble beauty by the ages broken:
  In all, thy love!

KINDRED

Musing, between the sunset and the dark,
  As Twilight in unhesitating lands
  Bore from the faint horizon's underlands,

Silvern and chill, the moon's phantasmal ark,
I heard the sea, and far away could mark
  Where that unalterable waste expands
  In sevenfold sapphire from the mournful sands,
And saw beyond the deep a vibrant spark.

There sank the sun Arcturus, and I thought:
  Star, by an ocean on a world of thine,
    May not a being, born, like me, to die,
Confront a little the eternal Naught
  And watch our isolated sun decline—
    Sad for his evanescence, even as I?

WINIFRED GRAY STEWART

Winifred Gray Stewart is a California writer who has
been widely published for a number of years. She is par-
ticularly notable for her apt and perceiving delineations of
nature, as in the sonnets that follow.

THEY ARE FOREWARNED

The little creatures of the under earth,
Alien to man, go their predestined ways:
In dusty tunnels they beget, give birth
And die. They live by darkness, and their days
Are barred with shade. Their narrow bodies flicker
Like darts of morning sunlight when they move.
My sudden step is quick; but they are quicker
Than winds that walk lightly from grove to grove.

And though by quiet patience I can tame them
To take the proffered morsel from my hand,
They are forewarned; and I shall never blame them

Because an immemorial command
Translates the tense and guarded tread as danger,
And man, at best, a brusque and sudden stranger.

ONLY THE ARROGANT HEART

Now at the end of summer stands the oak,
Letting without regret her gold leaves fall.
Here the dead pine awaits the ultimate stroke
Of wind to bring it low; and here is all
The beauty that was fern and flower and fruit
Withered and acquiescent; the first frost
Will find the imperfect seed, the cankered root;
Yet nothing shall be wasted, nothing lost.

Only the arrogant, proud heart of man
Rebels and shrinks at death's finality;
Comforts its failing self as best it can
With doubtful dreams of heavens yet to be;
Peers into Space, dickers with Time, yet dies
With troubled faith, less wise than trees are wise.

HELEN FRITH STICKNEY

Helen Frith Stickney is a New York poet, who has published widely in magazines and newspapers, and has written two books of verse: *Prelude to Winter*, a prize-winning entry in the Versecraft competition in 1933; and *Abigail's Sampler* (1943). She is on the Executive Board of the Poetry Society of America, and was for two years vice-president of that organization.

CAMOUFLAGE

This casual verdure, light and tremulous,
This bright complexity of swaying line,
Screens the artillery, but who would guess,
So innocent, so perfect the design.
Where leaf and shadow delicately trace
An arabesque, Nature has gladly shown
The artist how to memorize her face
And make her various patterns all his own.

Long has he listened to her silences,
Followed her every mood with indrawn breath,
Each soft, evasive gesture half unseen;
And she has given of herself for this—
That man should stare into the eyes of death,
Seeing a skull under the veil of green.

H. P. STODDARD

H. P. Stoddard, a lifelong resident of Washington, D. C.,
has contributed to various verse magazines, and is the author
of two books, *Fruit Unattainable* and *The Lips Keep Moving*.

THE SILENT COCKATOO

The iridescent trifle of a king,
   He preens beneath a cool hibiscus bower,
The flutter of his blue and yellow wing
   Dazzles the eye like some resplendent flower.
He splits the chilled heart of a gorgeous fruit,
   Flecking the creamy liquid with his claw;
He has no ponderous problems to compute;
   No consciousness of sin; no sense of awe.

Prismatic colors in an oval glass;
  The crystal greens within a lotus pool;
He sees these things, and, seeing, lets them pass:
  He has the weighty wisdom of a fool,
Who wisely knows that beauty's more acute,
When pens are dropped, and learnèd men are mute.

Leonora Clawson Stryker

Leonora Clawson Stryker, in early life, spent eleven years as a reporter and free-lance writer for New York and Buffalo newspapers, and at the same time contributed stories to the papers and magazines. For the past ten years she has confined herself to the writing of poetry, which has appeared in numerous periodicals. Formerly of Duluth, Minnesota, she lives today in Los Angeles.

PALPABLE SILENCE

So death-still are the hours, when you are gone,
So dully run the ancient hour-glass sands,
That waiting here, in this dim room, alone,
I almost touch the silence with my hands.

BOUNDLESS

Each finite thing has definite boundary;
The widest ocean ends on some far shore.
The soul, alone, remains a mystery,
Passing, unchallenged, every earthly door.

GALATEA TO PYGMALION

Day after day and far into the night
Your chisel wrought against my marble cell,

Until I was brought forth into the light
Of this strange world in which I am to dwell.
You fashioned me to suit your own desire,
An image out of that which was but stone,
Pressed on my silent lips your kiss of fire
That made of me a thing of flesh and bone.

And now that I am yours, Pygmalion,
Be gentle if I fail your passion's need
For I have not been wooed nor even won
Nor granted time to learn the lover's creed.
Be patient while I search the ways of men,
Lest I recede into the stone again.

JESSE STUART

One would have to go far to find a more "natural" poet
than Jesse Stuart—a poet whose writings, even if occasion-
ally a little roughshod, are more spontaneously the outpour-
ings of the heart. Like John Clare, of whom he is a not
unworthy successor, he springs directly from the soil, and
from childhood has helped plant and harvest crops; and, like
John Clare, he has a rich and profound feeling for the things
of the soil. Some years ago he was a "find" of the late John
Macrae of Dutton's, whose efforts elevated him into promi-
nence with an immediacy paralleled by few poets of modern
times. He is the author of two books of verse, three novels
and an autobiography; and has contributed to the *Atlantic,*
Harper's, Household, and other well-known magazines. He
was born in 1907 in Rivington, Kentucky, where he lived
until his recent entry into the United States Navy.

SONNETS FROM CAMP

I

I never knew before freedom could be
A little world of hills that I had known
Where I could get acquainted with a tree,
A sawbriar stool beside a lichened stone.
I never knew the song of April streams
Was sweeter music than the song of birds,
That old cocoons among the greenbriar stems
Did hold more magic than man's futile words.
I never knew how good it was to walk
In blowing wind beneath a roof of sky,
To hear the wind and tender oak leaves talk
Above my head as I went walking by,
Until first leave, nine days of liberty;
And then I knew how precious hours could be.

II

Some day we shall be going home to find
The weeds grown taller than our front yard gate,
Each window darkened by a lonely blind,
Dark eyeless cabin that's been left to fate
Except for wasps and bats beneath the eaves
And lizards running on the flagstone walk
And wind that rustles lazy dogwood leaves
Beneath whose shade our neighbors used to talk.
We'll give our cabin eyes to see again
When we return with chickens, dogs and cats;
We'll clean our grown-up fields for stalwart grain.
We'll clear the place of lizards, wasps, and bats.
Our chimney smoke will spiral on the air.
Old neighbors then will know that we are there.

III

Remember if this man is lost at sea
In feathery fathoms of its midnight deep

And waves can't break my brain's last secrecy
These will be images that I will keep:
High rugged hills that shouldered to the sun
When I went with my mother out to hoe
From early morn until the day was done
Light burley in the long tobacco row.
I'll keep old images of time and place,
Of redbud coves in fiery flakes of bloom,
Curve of Deane's lips, her hair, her handsome face,
Jane's playing with blocks in our living-room.
Eternal churning of the sea can't break
What I would sacrifice for freedom's sake.

KATHLEEN SUTTON

Kathleen Sutton is a native of Lowell, Massachusetts, but was transplanted at an early age to the Deep South of Anniston, Alabama, where she still lives. Her poems have appeared in the *Atlantic Monthly, Saturday Review of Literature, Free World*, etc. She is the author of two books and a brochure, as well as of short stories published in the experimental magazines and quarterlies. Her work is written with considerable verve and variety, and a good technical command of its material.

UNIVERSALISM

The earth is somnolent in the noon of its summer,
And I am one with the earth and the blade of grass
Cleaving the rock; I am one with the rock upholding
The tree, the fruit on the bough, and the sky's mute glass.

Nothing has been of which I am not all matter;
Smoke and lightning, steel, and the stain of blood

Laved by eternal tears. I am fear and hatred,
Lust and laughter and greed in an unstemmed flood.

Deeper than dust I have traced the course of the maggot;
Deeper than life, I have opened my soul and cried
For beauty as silent as moth wings that darkly hovered,
Brushing my eyes with sleep the morning I died.

Father and priest, and maiden to awed youth pledging
Fidelity by the timeless stars—I am these,
And shall be again. I am hope, and the soft lips suckling
A full, sweet breast . . . I am prayer . . . and old mem-
ories . . .

The earth is warm with summer. No wintry foreboding
Of neverness, more bitter than caustic mirth,
Disturbs the dream that is I—for waking or sleeping,
I am eternity—I am one with the earth!

GEESE FLYING OVER ENGLAND

("People watching below feared an air attack and hurried to
shelter."—*From a radio broadcast.*)

Geese, soaring arrow-sharp through thickening fog,
Look down with pity on those who watch far under!
Your flight resembles too nearly the dark prologue
To death's grim rain of thunder.

You are neither beauty now nor poetry;
(Though the heart perhaps recalls and stills its yearning
For a time when gray wings flying in curious V
Meant only the year's turning)

Lovely enough you are, and strong and wise
Above the trembling town. Oh, not of your making
Is the blood's chill, the panic blinding all eyes,
The heart's piteous quaking!

LONELY TRYST

Forgive me, heart, that of my own free will
I come again to the old trysting place;
That by the selfsame path I mount the hill
(Stars overhead, the wind against my face)
As once I climbed with Love, before the blow
Was struck, before the final word was said
That sent him reeling, plunging far below
To lie among the stones, broken and dead.

Forgive me, heart. It is not heedlessly
That I return, or as a murderer
Drawn by the scene of crime. But if there be
Pity in Heaven, let remembrance stir
The ghost of Love, that though it pass like mist,
We shall have kept this last, this lonely tryst.

ELDA TANASSO

Elda Tanasso was born October 23, 1917; was educated at
the College of New Rochelle and Columbia University; and
has published poems in the *New York Times, Poetry, Voices,
The Lyric,* and other periodicals. Her first collection of
verse, *The Dark Gaze,* appeared in 1944. She lives in Harrison, a suburb of New York.

REMEMBER THAT OUR LOVE MOVES LIKE THE SNOW

Remember that our love moves like the snow;
Softly as snow it comes upon the world;
It builds the air into a house impearled,
Corniced with forests where the still trees grow.

Remember now this whiteliness we know,
This individual peace, this gladness swirled
Richly around us; it is true; though hurled
In terror all the cold and wild winds blow.
Our hearts are calm; the snow is falling wide;
The world lies like a low-descended star;
And though our minds hear distantly the ride
Of heavy famine, pestilence, death, and war,
Our love moves like the snow and builds in pride
This hidden place with silence at the core.

SARA TEASDALE

Though her best work was published a quarter of a century ago, and though she·has been dead for over a decade, Sara Teasdale should properly be included in any consideration of the present group of poets. Her *Dark of the Moon* (1926) and *Strange Victory* (1933), no less than her *Collected Poems* (1937), have reinforced her place as a writer of tenuous, wistful and often appealingly graceful or deftly pointed songs, usually slight in content but able in presentation—songs that appear to have carved out for her a permanent place in the literature of simple lyricism.

Miss Teasdale was born in St. Louis in 1884, was educated in her home town, and spent much time in early life traveling in Europe and the Near East. In 1914 she married Ernst B. Filsinger, also a writer—but one whose field was foreign trade.

NOT BY THE SEA

Not by the sea, but somewhere in the hills,
Not by the sea, but in the uplands surely
There must be rest where a dim pool demurely
Watches all night the stern slow-moving skies;

Not by the sea, that never was appeased,
Not by the sea, whose immemorial longing
Shames the tired earth where even longing dies,
Not by the sea that bore Iseult and Helen,
But in a dark green hollow of the hills
There must be sleep, even for sleepless eyes.

WISDOM

It was a night of early spring,
  The winter-sleep was scarcely broken;
Around us shadows and the wind
  Listened for what was never spoken.

Though half a score of years are gone,
  Spring comes as sharply now as then—
But if we had it all to do
  It would be done the same again.

It was a spring that never came,
  But we have lived enough to know
What we have never had, remains;
  It is the things we have that go.

SISTER M. THÉRÈSE

Sister M. Thérèse, of the Congregation of the Sisters of
the Divine Savior, is the author of *Now There is Beauty* and
Give Joan a Sword, as well as of poems that have appeared
both in the religious and the lay press. Her work, while
often of a devout nature, occasionally strikes a more general
note with tenderness and imagination.

TO JOAN OF ARC ON D-DAY

Joan, be swift at the parapet,
There are long, dark shadows beneath the sun;
Snatch your shield from the wall of heaven,
With the grey of ships the waters run.

France is a-quiver with steel and shell
Pas-de-Calais to Brittany;
Rivet your armor and leave the sky
For the chalk cliffs slanting into the sea.

Have you not heard the voices, Joan?
They have pushed the gates of sky apart
And made all heaven lean to hear
The names we name with a kneeling heart.

Snatch your sword from its deep-worn sheaf,
The dark foe charges from hill and town;
His breath is flame on the Norman coasts,
Joan, be swift and smite him down!

Maid of the stanch and daring soul,
Stand with our men till the lands are free;
Haunt each lane in the cloud-hung heaven,
Sail each shining strip of sea.

Swear by the cross upon your breast,
Swear by the sword of Roncevalles,
That France shall rise, and peace shall lie
Like sun on the world's wide littoral.

NATHANIEL THORNTON

Nathaniel Thornton is Professor of English Literature and Abnormal Psychology, Abbe Institute, New York City; author of numerous poems, mostly sonnets, some of which have appeared in the *New York Times, New York Herald-Tribune, Spirit, Wings, The Lyric, Poetry Chap-book,* etc. He was formerly co-editor of *The Sonneteer,* a quarterly magazine; and is a lecturer on literary subjects and author of a group of critical essays on the English poets.

TO VIRGINIA WOOLF

That you, enamoured so of life and art,
And all the cherished memory of song,
Should darkly have decreed within your heart
That your own tenure had endured too long,
And, all intolerant of death's delay,
Have ached to share the fate of sands and rocks—
As though this only were the destined way—
Remains a veiled and rooted paradox.

But thus may some clairvoyance point the light
Which spurs the heart's clandestine enterprise;
"Why?" I am asking yet, as any might,
Though scarcely dare to shape a dim surmise.
And still the cautious Ouse makes no reply;
And still the earth is silent, still the sky.

LUCIA TRENT ·

Lucia Trent, daughter of Professor Emeritus William P. Trent of Columbia University, was born in Richmond, Virginia, and is a graduate of Smith College. She is co-author of four books with her husband Ralph Cheyney, who died in 1941; the two of them won considerable joint prominence by their mutual appearances in print and on the platform in the cause of poetry. She has recently re-married, and is living in San Antonio, Texas.

SALT TIDES

Here where the moonlight gleams like a fountain falling
In this familiar room our lives have shared
Our love is a quiet river-music calling.
We have forgot the ancient pain that glared.

But can we forget the griefs of the world that shatter,
The sneers as sharp as the beak of a savage bird,
Forget the million trivial things that matter,
The sparks that fly from the forge of a hasty word?

Through hidden oceans of mind now rising, now falling,
They live forever below our daily plane
And even when love is a river-music calling
There drift the tides of pain.

JOSEPH UPPER

Joseph Upper (Joseph U. Harris) is a District of Columbia writer, whose work for many years has been appearing in the poetry magazines. He is the author of one book of verse, *Walking Shadow*. The quatrain reprinted below was the winner of first prize in a national contest in 1936, having been selected out of more than twenty-five hundred entries.

ARTIST

I think October must have loved in vain.
    How otherwise can she portray such grief,
Painting with crimson or with yellow stain
    A whole life's story on a falling leaf?

OCTOBER PRELUDE

The sumacs burn beside the country lane,
Like sentenced prisoners who are to die.
Defiant in defeat, with their last sigh
They flaunt the scarlet gaiety of pain.
Throughout the night the clamor of the rain
And lightning flashes that torment the sky
Repeat the warning of the wild birds' cry:
"Death, surnamed Winter, soon will come again!"
Who faces Winter with no hope of Spring
Will seize the gift of each uncertain hour,
And tilt the goblet of diminished power
To gulp the dregs of cold imagining.
    The hectic challenge of his dying smile
    Recalls the sumacs flaming by the stile.

JUDY VAN DER VEER

On a ranch near Lakeside, an hour's drive inland from
San Diego in Southern California, Judy Van der Veer lives
in a world populated with cows, horses and sheep. Of these
she has written with an eloquent simplicity in her prose
books, *River Pasture* and *Brown Hills;* and with these also
she is mainly concerned in her poetry, which is unique of its
kind, a pure rill of spontaneous song, in which she deals with
the farm creatures and the wild things with a naturalness and

a deep pervasive sympathy that has been rarely equalled
and perhaps never surpassed in all the long history of poetry.

CALF IN THE GOLDENROD

I found a calf in the goldenrod,
Beside the sandy river;
I saw it lift its little head,
I saw its nostrils quiver.

The sky above was softly blue,
And the wild ducks were flying;
A lovely place to be born, I thought,
But a sorry place for dying.

For the old cow lay in the goldenrod,
And she would never rise;
She watched the little new-born calf
With big bewildered eyes.

And the breeze blew through the goldenrod,
And bent and swayed its head;
And the calf called to its mother,
—Nor knew that she was dead.

The sky above was softly blue,
And the wild ducks were flying;
A lovely place to be born, I thought,
But a sorry place for dying.

LITTLE WOODLAND GOD

I think that surely there's a god
For little, hunted things;
A god whose eyes watch tenderly
The droop of dying wings.

A little woodland god who sits
Beneath a forest tree,
With baby rabbits in his arms,
And squirrels on his knee.

And when a hunter bravely shoots
A deer with dreaming eyes,
I think that little god is there
To love it when it dies.

But all the hungry orphan things
Who weakly call and call—
For mothers who can never come.
He loves the best of all.

He tells the breeze to softly blow,
He tells the leaves to fall;
He covers little, frightened things
When they have ceased to call.

I think his pensive, Pan-like face
Is often wet with tears;
And that his little back is bent
From all the weary years.

COWS

They stand beside the pasture gate,
And wait, and softly low,
As cows stood by a pasture gate
A hundred years ago.

Up to the hills and down again
They wander on old trails;
But with the setting sun they come
Down to the pasture rails.

Oh, often I have heard them call
Throughout a night and day,
For little, soft-eyed calves that go
To markets far away.

And now beside the pasture gate
They wait, and softly low;
As cows stood by a pasture gate
A hundred years ago.

MARK VAN DOREN

Mark Van Doren requires no introduction to any American audience. Pulitzer Prize winner, author of eighteen or twenty books of poetry and criticism, literary editor of *The Nation* from 1924 to 1928, and Professor of English at Columbia University since 1935, he has been in the public eye time after time over a period of more than two decades. He was born in Hope, Illinois, in 1894, but has passed much of his life in New York City.

His poetry, which is marked by a certain severity and restraint and often by a cerebral quality, shows strongly the influence of Robert Frost and other members of the "New England School." Only occasionally—as in the piece quoted below—does the human factor in his work predominate

THE GOOD FATES

I see the dun, low western house,
I see the propless porch,
I see the grass and cherry-leaves
That a June sun would scorch;

While flies buzzed through the broken screen—
I hear one in the room,
I hear one settle on the plush
Past the piano's gloom.

Then silence in the forward part;
But there are doors and doors,
And deviously the clatter comes
Of middle summer's chores;

Of deep pots simmering on the fire,
Of strainers dropping juice;
Of knives; though most of all I hear
Three tongues upon the loose:

My aunt and her warm daughters there,
My cousins, whom I stand
Long years away and listen to
Across a changing land.

There is no sound has sung to me
Since then so rich a song;
So reticent of injury,
And yet so laughing strong;

So stopless; for the afternoon
Hangs high above us; waits
While their lost voices hum to me
Across these seven States;

Hum busily above the pans,
Unconscious how I hear
What he and she and Charlie did
In that fine cherry year.

HAROLD VINAL

Wherever contemporary American poetry is discussed, the name of Harold Vinal is known. For more than two decades he has edited one of our most prominent poetry journals, *Voices,* which he founded in 1921; and for a number of years he has been Secretary of the Poetry Society of America. Born in 1891 in Vinal Haven, Maine, where he still passes his summers, he has published seven volumes of verse and one of prose. The examples given below are fairly indicative of the quality of his poetry, which is essentially cerebral, eschews sentiment, and keeps its lyricism under sharp control.

PRESCIENCE

I

Who is vouchsafed to traffic with the truth
Shall need no graph or compass, for his mind
Has once explored reality, forsooth
Ranged the immortal ether unconfined.
Prodigious in his wisdom he shall be,
No longer waspish, and no longer mean,
Who has consorted with the spheres, for he
Has stripped the bandage from his eyes and seen.

Expect him not to gather up the dust
Of our mortality about his knees
Who, haloed and apart from time and rust,
Looks out beyond our littorals and sees,
As through the sudden opening of a door,
A vaster tide wash on a vaster shore.

II

Servile to time no longer, and beyond
The dull, lugubrious shadows of the earth,

He dwells serene in logic who has donned
The lighter garments of another birth.
What canticles sound in his ears we hear
But as an echo or a whisper thrown
Across our dreams, who in a web of fear
Walk unregenerate and walk alone.

Who sees the signet written on his brow
Shall through a lens of credence pierce the pale
Mirage of death, and for an instant bow
Before the loftier vision of the grail,
Wearing like him, the while our fingers grope,
The outer trappings of an inner hope.

SATAN IN PROFILE

Chagrined, because he saw us flitting past,
Like black-masked figures in a carnival,
He sat behind his arras, and, aghast,
Peered out at us and thought us tragical.
Much as a bored spectator at the zoo,
He looked upon our saturnalian play,
And wondered at us with his face askew,
As we all wondered at him in our way.

A little better than the average man,
He listened to our odd and golden lies,
Dreaming, perhaps, of Eld or Kubla Khan,
With something more than malice in his eyes.
Impeccable, above our glittering floor,
He sat like Satan, framed against the door.

BLANCHE SHOEMAKER WAGSTAFF

Blanche Shoemaker Wagstaff, author of some dozen books of verse, contributor to 150 anthologies, winner of many literary prizes, and a critic, dramatist and translator of Greek classics, is familiar to all who have followed American letters over a period of years. Her latest book is *The Beloved Son* (1944). She was born in 1888 in New York City, where she still lives.

PILGRIMAGE

For each of us a different path to God,
   The poet by the starway of his dreams
    Or yet perhaps the sound of singing streams
May lead to hidden pinnacles untrod.
The lover finds in love the magic rod
   Which wafts him upward. and a beauty gleams
    Sometimes in strange and unseen ways. It seems
We go our way upon the flowering sod

Seeking forever an invisible goal,
   For deeper beauty always hungering,
    Yet never nearing the desired height,
For hidden it waits beyond us, and the whole
   Of life is but a pilgrimage, to wring
    From chaos one star burning in the night.

FRANCES REVETT WALLACE

Frances Revett Wallace, who was born in San Francisco in 1900 and was educated there at Miss Burke's School and at the California School of Fine Arts, has painted since childhood, but began writing poetry in the late Thirties, when for a few years she was too ill to crawl up two flights of studio stairs. She has contributed to the magazines, and has one book, *The Chinaware of Dreams*.

ONLY THEN . . .

Within the silence of a cloistered court
I found an agèd nun beneath whose veil
A face of pale serenity gazed forth,
Like ivoried parchment in an ancient book.
I asked her to define eternity,
And to my plaint that it was measureless
Beyond all concepts of the human mind,
Her wisdom gave this strange analogy:
"If you should hang a ball in space," she said,
"The earth's own size, yet metal to the core,
And every thousand years a swallow's wing
Should brush it till the ball were worn away,
Eternity would only then begin."
And as she spoke, I knew that I had seen,
Behind the shadows in her lonely eyes,
The timeless peace that is eternity.

TESSA SWEAZY WEBB

Tessa Sweazy Webb has long been associated with American poetry: for thirteen years she conducted a reprint column, "Voices and Echoes," in the *Columbus* (Ohio) *Sunday Dispatch;* and simultaneously for eleven years she wrote a prose column, "With the Poets," for the same paper. She is editor of *The Singing Quill,* a quarterly magazine of verse; is the author of numerous magazine poems, and of two collections of verse; is the founder of Ohio Poetry Day;

and has collaborated with the Ohio Department of Education in compiling two anthologies of verse for public school use.

LOVE'S UNVEILING

There was a time I watched with fortitude
The burnished stars that flecked the night with gold,
Wondering if love's eyes would ever hold
Such glittering fires, when once the heart reviewed
Its broken dreams. Would autumn's fog-dim mood
Forget the glamour May had aureoled?
And winter past, would April airs unfold
Their loveliness in warm green fields renewed?

The stars were silent, while the exacting years
Have wrought their meed of pleasure and of pain,
Given bitter for the sweet and loss for gain.
My dreams are cloistered now. I have no fears.
For watching love so quietly come and go,
The wonder is departed. Now I know!

Mary Weeden

Mary Weeden (Mary Weeden Stiver) was born in 1909 on a farm in Southern Ohio, graduated from Michigan State Normal College, and is at present living in Richmondville, New York. Her poems have appeared in *Household Magazine* and in the verse magazine *Trails*.

THE STEEP SLOPES OF MORNING

Up the steep slopes of morning
The years pass single file,
And man was born to follow
From the least to the furthest mile.

Up the steep slopes of morning
To the high white peaks of noon,
Man knows the miles are passing
But the bright sun dims the moon.

Beyond the slopes of morning
On the shadowed side of noon,
Man wakes to full awareness
That the night comes all too soon.

Edward Weismiller

Recipient of an award in the Yale Series of Younger Poets at the age of twenty-one, Edward Weismiller has differed from many prize-winners in not slipping back into obscurity; his poems have continued to appear at intervals since his original recognition in 1936. He was born in Wisconsin; was educated at Swarthmore and at Cornell College, Iowa; and gathered the material for his book *The Deer Come Down* while living on a farm near Brattleboro, Vermont. The sonnets quoted below are the opening ones of the title sequence.

THE DEER COME DOWN

I

Softly, by night, the deer come down to drink
At the secret pools, at the curve of the hidden streams;
Their eyes no longer bright with easy dreams
The deer come to strange water. There at the brink
They lean out of the thickets: not as they stood
In safer times; their cool immaculate mouths
Move in the shallows, quenching their day-long drouths
Swiftly before they leap for the comfortless wood.

They are an exiled people, running the trails
From their green whispering towns. Even by day
You will hear their footfalls softer and farther away
In the forests; while the cold, bright northern sun
Leaps in their fearful eyes, and their breathing fails,
And the wind beats in at their ears: you are lost, you are
    done.

II

O cities, you have nudged at their velvet flanks
With stony arms: and now in the throbbing dawn
If you cup your ears to the wind, if you look, they are gone,
With no print under the beeches or on wet banks
To show which way they went. Out of the ground
You sucked the water away from their shy thirst
To wash your metal hands; they are gone, now, cursed,
And all that is left is the wind and the running sound.

You sucked their breathing angrily under your tongues,
Cities, you laid your spittle upon their path
And scorched their isolate eyes with a new-learned wrath;
When the deer came down to drink, to the water-bed,
You pressed your poisonous breath upon their lungs
And burst their eyes with light; now they have fled.

BURIAL

I have heard the foxes,
when everything was still,
lost and wild and squalling
off behind the hill,
(the dark wind breathing
a subtle taint of musk,
and wild rose petals
shaking in the dusk.)
I have picked my gun up,

and slipped to where they pass
with dainty little footsteps
weaving through the grass;
and when the world was quiet
and the grass stained red
I have seen the foxes—
   the sly and tawny foxes—
     the little, grinning foxes—
lying still and dead.

When *I* die, defend me
with no earthen mound
(the wild rose petals
wither on the ground);
cover me but lightly
with leaves and yellow grass,
and let the little foxes
see me as they pass.
This be the burial
of him who loves and kills:
I would have them eat my heart
and scuttle to the hills;
and when my eyes fall open,
brimming with the rain,
I will see the foxes—
   the slim and tawny foxes—
     the little hungry foxes—
stealing here, again.

WINIFRED WELLES

During the comparatively few years of her life, Winifred
Welles won a reputation as one of America's leading women
poets. She was born in Norwich Town, Connecticut, on

January 26, 1893, and died on November 22, 1939; and published five books of verse, in addition to some prose and verse for children, her latest volume being the posthumous *The Shape of Memory* (1944). Her work has a delicate and sometimes sprightly quality; while rarely penetrating in its insight, it is often touched with quaint and appealing fancies, and with that exquisite "brushing of wings" that is one of the surest if least definable tests of a poet.

GOLDEN OUTLINE

Not only heads are haloed, nor are faces
   The only thin, transparent masks for light.
There are clear landscapes, coasts of crystal, places
   As finely frail, as perilously slight
As gossamer, and through them glistens faintly
The secret country, luminous and saintly.

Sometimes I stand so close to that rich center,
   That, exquisitely scorched by its rich core,
I think, now in a moment I can enter. . . .
   But in that moment all the fire-grained shore,
The coals along the hills are darkening, failing,
And I am still this side the silver veiling.

TWANGING GOLD

I hear, far up the mountain trail,
Like some dim instrument in sleep,
With tarnished strings and taut and frail,
The voices of a thousand sheep,
A sweet, distraught and fragile wail.
From all those tightened little throats,
The huddle of white beasts, it floats,
A chant of innocence and tears,
Far down the mountain, down the years.
On acres biblical and bleak,

Through tinted pastures of the Greek,
From landscapes grey as tapestries,
Down sloping meadows edged with trees,
Flocks as forlorn as this have cried.
I hear, upon the mountain side,
Borne through the bright air, blurred and faint,
The same, queer, exquisite complaint
As shepherd-king and hermit-saint. . . .
It's like a warped harp twanging gold,
Jangled, gentle, and ages old.

John T. Westbrook

Normally a university instructor in English, John T. West-brook has for the past several years served as soldier and farmer, though meanwhile his poems have continued to appear in various places, including the *American Mercury* and the better-known "little magazines." His present address is Greenwell Springs, Louisiana.

SUMMER BAYOU

Here slow suns burned down stifling afternoons
How many eons in a sky like this?
What dateless light of Mesozoic moons
Rose here and set when mind was chrysalis?

How many winds from sterile snows grown old
Greened rainy changes in the wombing spring?
What yellow life dropped here to meet the mould
Through ancient days of death and blossoming?

Now shadows stagnate in an air so still
It might have slept an age in glacial rime

Intact, tuned to one deathless whippoorwill
From a lost summer in the dawn of time.

Here thoughts aghast at war find deep surcease,
Blue in a breezeless pool of crystal peace.

KATHARINE WELLES WHEELER

Katharine Welles Wheeler, of Tacoma, Washington, is the author of one book, *Filled Flagons*, and of many magazine verses. Although she is a western woman, she has spent a number of years in the East, studying art and music.

THE CIRCLE

Out of the boundless firmament there whirled
This pattern rim of all the wheels of Time;
It shaped the hub . . . the nave whereon the world
Vibrates to tones incomparable, sublime.
Its radial span encompasses the moon . . .
The heavens where synchronizing stars are spun . . .
The glorious nimbus of the sun at noon;
It is a miracle of law begun.
There in the primal dawn it came to be,
Rolling . . . rolling on to Eternity.

JOHN HALL WHEELOCK

The year 1905 marked the first tentative burgeoning of two notable literary figures, John Hall Wheelock and Van Wyck Brooks, whose *Verses by Two Undergraduates* appeared in that year. Mr. Wheelock, then a student at Harvard aged but nineteen, was to follow this fledgling effort with six other books before the collected *Poems* of 1936, and was to take his place among the most widely known American poets. He has served for years on the editorial staff of Charles Scribner's Sons. His work, faithful to the best lyrical traditions, is marked by that grace of expression and that emotional element so frequently lacking in contemporary verse.

SEA VOYAGE

To what dark purpose was the will employed
    That fashioned, ere the dawn of time grew dim,
    The waste of ocean—from clear rim to rim
A crystal chamber, sorrowful and void?

For, surely, not without design He wrought
    These vast horizons on whose margins rest
    The extremes of heaven, nor from east to west
Widened the waters to the bounds of thought.

Half-hopeful, half-incredulous, I wait
    For some gigantic presence to assume
    His throne, in the large circle of the room,
The dreadful distances are desolate.

In vain! In vain! He is departed hence,
    Whose breath troubles the waters of the sea:
    Twilight and night are sworn to secrecy,
The heavens preserve their ancient innocence.

In the enormous throne-room of the sun
    No voice is audible. The waves are mute.
    Solitude, infinite and absolute,
Bears witness to the unreturning One.

Evening, on the lorn reaches of the sea,
  Comes vast and patient; but the night is kind—
  Her hand is pity, scarfing up the blind
Sorrows and wastes of the immensity.

The wind is soft among the swaying spars.
  Heaven deepens; dusk reveals the glittering height
  And cloudless glory of the arch of night,
Bowed down from rim to rim with solemn stars.

When dawn across the broad and billowing plain
  Casts her pale fire, the monstrous solitude
  Of huddling waters—the old hope renewed—
Thrills with blind love, and yearns, but all in vain.

Sheer to the east, sheer to the west extend,
  Far as the wandering wings of thought may grope,
  The eternal vacancies. No hope, no hope—
Distance, distance forever, without end.

Hour by hour, and day on burning day,
  Our vessel plows the soft, reluctant foam;
  Hour by hour, and mile on mile, we roam
The lonely and the everlasting way.

Still fades before us the enormous round—
  Blue sea below, blue heaven overhead—
  The Void, eternal and untenanted,
A chamber for His splendor, without bound.

MARGARET WIDDEMER

Poet, novelist and short story writer, Margaret Widdemer
began writing in childhood; first won recognition for the

widely quoted social poem, *The Factories;* and has since
turned out many books both of prose and verse, won many
literary honors, and been active in the councils of the
Authors' League of America, the Poetry Society of America,
and the Poets' Guild of Christadora House. Her poetry,
which at its best shows both delicacy of utterance and imag-
ination, has of recent years been largely subordinated to her
prose. Her home is in Larchmont, New York.

DIALOGUE

I

One Speaks from Earth

How dare you be so far, whose arms surrounded,
    Whose face pressed mine, whose body held mine fast?
Can I come home to you when all is vanished,
    Will you be in the Timeless at the last?

I can bear distance from your unknown dwelling,
    And walk alone these dry and hopeless ways
If after all the miles of dark and sorrow
    You lift a latch for me at end of days:

Be still the soul that keeps my soul: the arrow
    That strikes the mark of me;
Be gift of death—be heart of darkness only;
    Somewhere exist! Somewhere await and be!

II

One Speaks from Heaven

Take this, the promise of the long-forgotten,
    Long waited for:
You are alone; yet where your lone door closes
    I close the door.

I come to you who do not know me coming;
  What is your peace but this, your calm but this,
Your laughter I who touch across the spaces,
  Your passion my far touch, your joy my kiss?

I am your quietness; I am your pleasure;
  I shall go always burning at your side.
Where I stand waiting you in Everlasting,
  My arms stand wide.

B. Y. WILLIAMS

B. Y. Williams (Mrs. Karl H. Williams) is co-founder
and co-editor with Annette Patton Cornell of *Talaria,* one of
the better known quarterlies of verse, which has been ap-
pearing since 1936. She is the author of four books of poetry,
the winner of numerous literary awards, and a contributor
to magazines such as *Saturday Evening Post, Ladies' Home
Journal,* etc. Her home is in Cincinnati.

LIKE FLAKES OF SNOW

The words fell from your lips like flakes of snow—
  So cool, so light, so gentle. By what art
Of transmutation can words spoken so
  Beat heavily as stones upon the heart!

SONNET IN SORROW

Austere and lovely Vega, you have gazed
  For countless ages on the griefs of men!
Serene you meet despairing eyes upraised
  In wonder that the stars can shine again!

Have you no pity for the hearts new-torn,
  No sign of comforting to still the cry
When sorrow seems too heavy to be borne,
  No answer to the old, old question, "Why?"

Comes there a morning, Vega? Did the power
  That fixed your calm blue splendor overhead
Think thus to hold our faith the little hour
  Until the darkness of our night be fled?
Is there a balm for grief? It must be so,
Else would your light have faded long ago!

CELESTE TURNER WRIGHT

A native of Maine but a resident of California since the
age of twelve, Celeste Turner Wright is Associate Professor
of English and Chairman of the Division of Languages and
Literature of the University of California College of Agricul-
ture at Davis. Her publications include research in Eliza-
bethan literature and poems in numerous magazines, some
of which have been widely noted; she has written capable
lyrics, but has shown a particular individuality and skill in
her handling of the sonnet form.

THUMBPRINT

Almost reluctant, we approach the block
Cleft from a stout sequoia; calculate
By arches, loops, concentric rings the date
Of Hastings, Plymouth, Gettysburg. The shock
Darkens our eyes; as dying men a clock,
We read the scornful summary of fate—
Elizabeth an inch—and estimate
How such curtailment at our love shall mock.

Redwood has fingerprinted Time, the seams
Of his gigantic thumb: this circlet grew
While Heloise yet laughed; these whorls define
Dante's "new life"; and when this curve was new,
John Keats could hope for mercy. Shall our dreams
Shrink to a millimeter, half a line?

TODAY

The best of life is nearest: he who grieves
Because the past was sweet, too late shall learn
That vanished summer's withered, fragrant leaves,
Loved overmuch, to mournful ashes turn;
And he who longs and yearns to see how bright
With opal tints tomorrow's dawn will be
Can never know with what a glorious light
The sun this evening sought the western sea.

No softer breeze perhaps has ever blown
Than that which makes my plane tree sway and bow,
And no more fragrant rose has ever grown
Than that which blossoms in your garden now.
Rise before loveliness has slipped away,
And open wide your arms to clasp Today!

ELINOR WYLIE

One of the most celebrated of American women poets,
Elinor Wylie was born in New Jersey in 1885, but subse-
quently lived in Washington, D. C., and in New York, where
in 1923 she married William Rose Benét. She began writing
only at the age of thirty-five, but in the few years preceding
her death in 1928 she produced four novels in addition to
several books of poems. Her work, even if at times a little

remote and lacking in warmth, is remarkably individualized, graceful, polished and imaginative.

SLEEPING BEAUTY

Imprisoned in the marble block
  Lies Beauty; granite in her dress;
The strong may carve from living rock
  A lady like a lioness.

With hammer blow and chisel cut
  They make the angry Beauty leap.
For me the obdurate stone is shut;
  How shall I wake her from her sleep?

An acorn tossed against an oak,
  A hazel wand that turns—and look!
She parts the leaves, a pearly smoke,
  She cleaves the earth—a silver brook.

SONNET

You are the faintest freckles on the hide
Of fawns; the hoofprint stamped into the slope
Of slithering glaciers by the antelope;
The silk upon the mushroom's under side
Constricts you, and your eyelashes are wide
In pools uptilted on the hills; you grope
For swings of water twisted to a rope
Over a ledge where amber pebbles glide.

Shelley perceived you on the Caucasus;
Blake prisoned you in glassy grains of sand
And Keats in goblin jars from Samarcand;
Poor Coleridge found you in a poppy-seed;
But you escape the clutching most of us,
Shaped like a ghost, and imminent with speed.